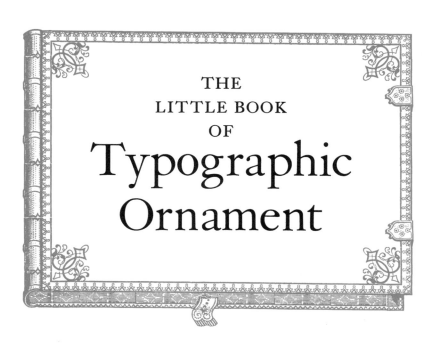

THE
LITTLE BOOK
OF
Typographic
Ornament

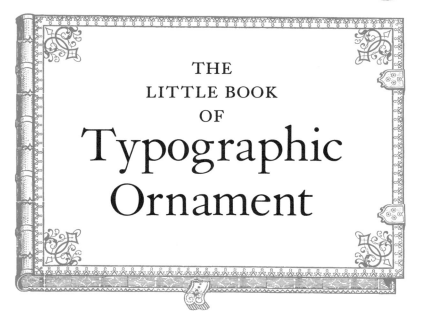

THE
LITTLE BOOK
OF
Typographic
Ornament

Published in 2015 by
Laurence King Publishing Ltd
361–373 City Road
London EC1V 1LR
Tel: +44 20 7841 6900
Fax: +44 20 7841 6910
Email: enquiries@laurenceking.com
www.laurenceking.com

A catalogue record for this book is available
from the British Library.

ISBN 13: 978 1 78067 589 3

Designed by Alexandre Coco and Jason Ribeiro;
based on an original concept by Angus Hyland,
Pentagram Design

Printed in China

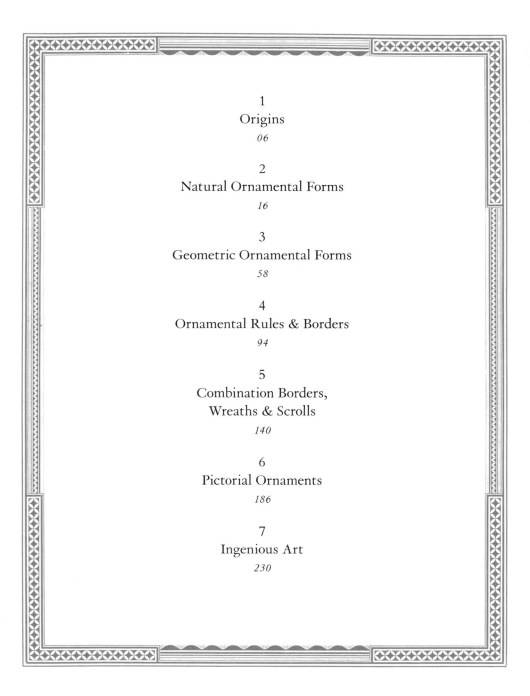

1
Origins

Ornament is something quite separate from the functional form of an object or printed information. If you are not sure if something is purely ornamental, then just imagine what would happen if it were not there. If the information or object continues to function as it should, then the feature is ornamental.[1]

Ornament, therefore, is intended to provide something over and above what is strictly necessary. Since ornament is not constrained by the needs of function in any physical sense, the artist, designer or craftsman can flex his or her imaginative and manipulative skills to the full. In the end, the only restriction is the imagination of the craftsman or, more likely, the client's budget.

Fig. 1

*Decorated border,
Monotype Rope, early
twentieth century.*

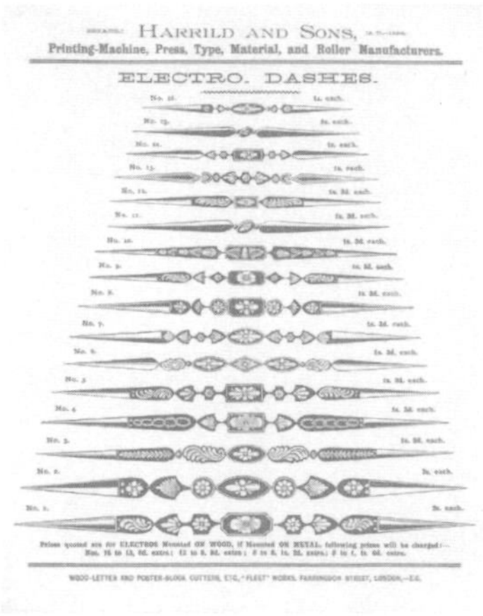

HARRILD AND SONS,

Printing-Machine, Press, Type, Material, and Roller Manufacturers.

ELECTRO. DASHES.

Fig. 2

*Ornamental rules, also
referred to as 'dashes', Harrild
and Sons type foundry, London,
1906.*

This book offers a brief historic overview of typographic ornament and a generous number of examples, the earliest from about 1557 and the last from 2014. Although these ornaments have been allotted to certain chapter titles, it will be appreciated that there are a significant number that could comfortably appear within two, three or indeed *any* of the chapters. It is hoped that these examples will provide inspiration for further exploration and development.

Most of the typographic ornaments displayed in this book are taken from the specimen books of type foundries from Europe, Great Britain and America. It was from these publications (the earliest being by William Caslon, London, dated 1734) that printers would order new fonts of type and typographic ornaments right up until the arrival of digital technology in the 1980s.

Typographic ornaments take several forms. The simplest kinds of ornament are *rules*, which print as a plain, uninterrupted straight line. They were made of strips of brass and available in a variety of thicknesses; they could also be cut to any length. Multiple rules, where two or more lines of the same or differing widths were on the same metal strip, were also common (as used to frame this page).

A *border* is a repeated decorative design (fig. 1) cast on a single strip of any length, exactly like that of the rule. However, a border can also be constructed from various individual printers' ornaments or 'printers' flowers'. The wide range of *swelled* or *tapered rules* (also, misleadingly, referred to as 'dashes'), whose length is fixed by their design, are also described as *ornamental rules* (fig. 2).

Printers' flowers (or *fleurons*) are quite different. These are individual decorative units designed to be arranged into variably shaped areas of decoration. They can also be arranged to form borders and so are sometimes, inaccurately, referred to as 'border units' rather than flowers.

The term 'flower' is generic and is used to describe all printers' individual units of decorative ornamental material, despite the fact that many are not, in fact, flowers or even representative of natural forms (fig. 3). Nor are these typographic ornaments limited to the purely ornamental. For example, 'acorns' and 'fists' (many of the more common flowers have specific names of their own) have a long tradition of use as signifiers within texts. One of the oldest typographic ornaments is the 'hedera leaf' [❧], also known as a 'floral heart', which is used as an inline character to divide paragraphs, similar to the 'pilcrow' or 'paragraph mark' [¶].

❧

From the outset, ornament has played an important role in the appearance of printed material, and especially the design of books. The earliest examples of printed decorative borders were made from hand-engraved strips of wood during the 1470s, some 20 years after Gutenberg's invention of printing from moveable metal type. Printers' flowers – individual metal units – were developed from the brass stamps (fig. 4) that had been used by bookbinders to decorate the leather-clad covers of books for many centuries.

Fig. 3

Cover design by Claud Lovat Fraser, Apropos the Unicorn, Curwen Press, London, 1920.

Fig. 4

A twentieth-century bookbinder's stamp, made from brass.

It was only natural that printers would seek to use similar designs to add typographic ornament to the pages inside the book, especially the title page. One of the earliest books in which typographic ornament was printed from individual printers' flowers is Henri Estienne's *Quincuplex Psalterium*, Paris, 1509.

Despite the pride so clearly taken in the display of typographic ornament, historic information regarding the development of the printers' flower is scarce. Many of the famous printing manuals, for example Fertel (1723); Fournier (1742 and 1768); Luckombe (1771); and Johnson (1824), include examples of vignettes, flowers and decorative rules, but none of these concern themselves with their origins. Typically, Fournier's two-volume *Manuel Typographique* of 1764[2] provides 31 pages of flower specimens and, indeed, he uses them with great finesse throughout his book, but he offers nothing about their history or development or, indeed, how to set about using them.[3]

What is certain is that the initial design of individual printers' flowers was strongly influenced by the culture and craftsmanship emanating from the East. Although the invention of printing from moveable type had been made in Mainz, Germany, c. 1450–55, it was Venice, effectively the gateway linking Europe and the East, which became the most celebrated and productive centre for printing from around 1470. Here, the skill of the oriental craftsmen, especially in metalwork, pottery, embroidery and weaving, was much admired, and Arabian craftsmen established clusters of workshops in many cities throughout Italy. Such was the interest in oriental craftsmanship that books solely containing oriental pattern designs were printed between 1500 and 1550, and their contents shamelessly copied by printers across Europe. Arabian design became intrinsic to Renaissance printing.

By the end of the seventeenth century the formal aesthetics of the Renaissance and the repeated copying of classical styles began to give way to something less predictable and restrained. The exuberance of the Baroque and then Rococo styles was immediately and universally popular, but nowhere more so than in Louis XV's France, where rich and frivolous decoration was applied to everything: walls, furniture, jewellery and, of course, books.

The eighteenth century was a remarkable period of regeneration and refinement in the use of typographic ornament. Earlier specimens were carefully redrawn and re-cut and many new designs were created. The *livre de luxe* or 'deluxe book' swiftly became one of the established extravagances of the age. Initially, most of the lavish ornamental work these books contained was provided by engravers, who supplied not only individual illustrations but also headbands, tailpieces and entire title pages, complete with hand-drawn lettering. Nicolas Cochin (1715–90) was perhaps the greatest of these graphic artists.

Not surprisingly, the foremost letterpress printers of the day strived to lessen the influence of the engravers. However it was Pierre-Simon Fournier 'le Jeune' (1712–68), a type founder in Paris, who so expertly applied the Rococo style to the design of type and typographic ornament, offering the printer a level of freedom and expression never experienced before. By 1742 Fournier had cut an enormous number of printers' flowers, as well as vignettes and borders in this new style and, in so doing, he potentially freed the letterpress printer from the services of the engraver (fig. 5). The era most celebrated for the use and development of typographic ornament had begun. Flourishes, blown-out corner pieces, florid borders, shell-work, flower baskets and all manner of ornaments could be built up from elements designed by Fournier. These creations were copied all over France and, indeed, much of Europe. Throughout the eighteenth century, typographic ornaments gained popularity, their complex, elegant patterns being equated with sophistication – a virtue coveted above all else by the high-street retailer for whom a reputation for finesse and service was paramount.

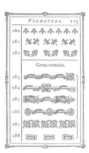

Fig. 5

*Pierre-Simon Fournier,
vignettes from the first volume
of* Manuel Typographique,
Paris, 1764.

Most celebrated of those influenced by Fournier was the young Giambattista Bodoni (1740–1813) in Parma, Italy. The first of his two celebrated type specimen books, *Fregi e majuscole* (two volumes), 1771, contains many typographic ornaments, some of which are virtually identical to those designed by Fournier. However, over time, Bodoni's types and ornaments took on a less exuberant appearance (fig. 6), reflecting a renewed general interest in classical history, resulting from the reported excavations of Pompeii and Herculaneum and the public exhibitions that followed. In his second specimen book, *Manuale Tipografico*[4], produced during the last few years of his life (and published posthumously), Bodoni went further by limiting himself almost exclusively to simple rules for typographic ornament. Others however, most notably Joseph-Gaspard Gillé in Paris, continued to produce a huge quantity of traditional, decorative neoclassical or 'modern antique' flowers, vignettes, borders and rules, as well as decorative or 'fancy' letters.

Within the confines of the printers' workshop – unfortunately, not *always* a place of pride and integrity as decreed by the printers' guilds – compositors often held printers'

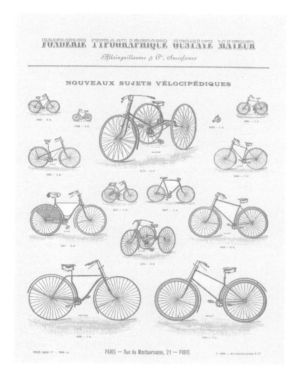

Fig. 7

*Stock images of bicycles,
Gustave Mayeur type foundry,
Paris, 1900.*

Fig. 8

*Title page of the type specimen
catalogue of MacKellar,
Smiths & Jordan, 1888. The
central panel carrying the
words 'Letter Founders' uses
the typeface Arboret 2.*

flowers in little affection. The severity of working conditions together with piece-rate working practices meant that those compositors who lacked the necessary experience would, if possible, avoid using them. Philip Luckombe, in his *The History of Art and Printing*, London, 1771, explains the situation thus: 'It is feared that … flowers will not long continue either in England, France or Germany, considering that the contriving and making them up is attended with considerable trouble and loss of time; and as no allowance is made for this it will not be strange if but few shall be found who will give instances of their fancy.' (p. 284).

Fig. 9

Bruce Rogers, title page of
The Ballad of William
Sycamore, *Edmond Byrne
Hackett, New York, 1923.*

By the beginning of the nineteenth century, improvements in the engineered sophistication of printing presses, together with improved knowledge of metallurgy, enabled type and ornaments to be designed more easily, incorporating ever finer, more delicate lines. These technical advances were part and parcel of the Industrial Revolution, which, significantly for the printer, also led to a dramatic increase in large-scale manufacturing. Now, printed matter in the form of labels, handbills, posters and business stationery, as well as notices and advertisements in newspapers and magazines, were all-important for the burgeoning manufacturing industries. The printer was forced to delve into his type cases with a view to using type and ornament as a means of attracting the attention of the viewer.[5] This demand was met by the type foundries who, from 1815, began devising a new generation of bolder, more flamboyant and characterful typefaces and ornaments designed specifically for the needs of advertising.

A little later, in 1839, another technical innovation called stereotyping enabled foundries to manufacture duplicates of any given ornament very cheaply. The same process was used to provide a huge variety of 'stock' images such as ships, houses, trains, farm animals, and later bikes and cars, to satisfy the demands of newspaper and magazine advertisers (fig. 7). This spawned a whole new line of business for engravers who were commissioned by type foundries to produce images that were converted into blocks called 'stereos' or 'electros' in large quantities and sold through their catalogues to printers. Some foundries, especially in America, specialized in this kind of material, and their catalogues – the 'image banks' of their time – often held many thousands of images from which the printer could choose.

During the nineteenth century, American heavy engineering industries became increasingly influential and American type foundries, having begun by copying the popular fonts and ornaments of British and European foundries, were, by the 1860s, truly innovating. One of the most influential of these was MacKellar, Smiths & Jordan, based in Philadelphia (fig. 8). Although primarily a maker of type, the company also supplied anything else that printers might need, including presses and other related tools and machinery. The huge scale of manufacturing by such foundries, as well as their global reach, was changing the very nature of the printers' craft. In fact, many considered the apparently irresistible allure of decorative material, or 'instant art', proffered by companies such as MacKellar, Smiths & Jordan, to be proof that the craft of the compositor was already dead.

In the 1890s an international print revival was instigated, but, significantly, not by the printing fraternity itself. Initially inspired by William Morris's magnificent (but expensive and exclusive) Kelmscott Press books (1891–6), a new generation of designers, passionate about printing and typography, wanted to utilize the new and much improved printing and typesetting technology while rejuvenating a sense of pride and craftsmanship in the printing trade. The leading practitioners of this loosely aligned movement were Bruce Rogers (fig. 9), working for the Riverside Press in Cambridge, USA; Anton Kippenberg and Carl Ernst Poeschel at Insel Verlag in Leipzig, Germany; and Francis Meynell (fig. 10), first at the Pelican Press, then at the Nonesuch Press in London. However, the aims of the print revival were best demonstrated by the output of the remarkable Curwen Press in London between 1920 and 1940 (fig. 3). With Claud Lovat Fraser, Percy Smith, Eric Ravilious and Edward Bawden among the prodigious number of freelance designers it employed (together with Oliver Simon overlooking its creative direction and Harold Curwen responsible for printing standards), the company provided a newly designed and strikingly fresh range of printers' flowers, vignettes, borders and illustrations aimed at the needs of the twentieth-century printer. This, however, proved to be the last resurgence of typographic ornament, until the arrival of digital technology provided designers with the means to devise decorative material of their own creation.

Fig. 10

Francis Meynell, title page of A Plurality of Worlds, *Nonesuch Press, London, 1929.*

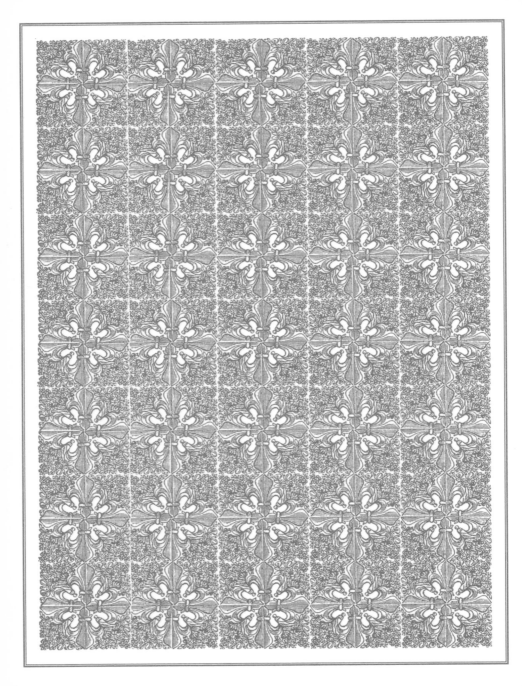

2
Natural Ornamental Forms

The large majority of typographic ornaments incorporate design elements derived from natural forms: this is also, no doubt, the reason for their generic term, 'printers' flowers'. The geographic and cultural origin of an early style of printers' flower is reflected in their being commonly described as 'arabesques', that is, Arabian. This is slightly misleading because some of these early ornaments were also based on ancient Roman decorations. Nevertheless, by the seventeenth century 'arabesque' was a commonly used term to describe *any* symmetrical design that included intertwining or sinuous lines representing the natural forms of, for example, grasses, leaves and branches (fig. 1).

Fig. 1

*Arabesque flowers, this design
made from four metal units.
Originating in Lyon or
Antwerp, not later than 1557.*

Fig. 2

*Simple yet infinitely
extendable Arabic geometric
motif, c. 1550.*

The relationship between Islamic geometry and the design of Renaissance-period typographic ornament is symbiotic, combining the authority of Classicism with the ebullience of Islamic design. The concept of ornament being infinitely extendable beyond the space it actually occupies on the page is emblematic of Islamic art. Typically, there is no attempt at realism in either; no particular species of plant is represented and the forms depicted are often botanically implausible. Islamic beliefs also caused the depiction of animals and people to be discouraged, which explains the tendency towards abstraction and, in turn, geometric pattern (fig. 2).

The arrival of the Rococo period during the eighteenth century with its rich, freer-flowing, elaborate architectural decoration also influenced the design of printed matter, especially with regard to typographic ornament. Most significant by far were Pierre-Simon Fournier's innovative designs, which effectively transferred the freedom of the engraver's tools in creating ornate letters and decorative swashes to metal type and the letterpress printer's press (fig. 3). In so doing, Fournier invited the compositor to compose in a far more original way. His flowers offered the opportunity to set ornaments into intricate filaments, often including swirling S and C scrolls, rather than the more formal and static square and circle. Rococo design was often not symmetrical (fig. 4) in that one half of the design did not always mirror the other half, and, although Fournier never went quite this far, his use of typographic ornaments certainly represents a dramatic break from the more formal work of the Renaissance printers. The decorative excess of the Rococo period, especially among the French monarchy, together with the luxury and glamour it represented, was brought to a sudden and violent end with the French Revolution of 1789.

The French Revolution caused the dispersal of French art, furniture and other decorative objects, and it was thus that the distinctive character of Rococo decoration – albeit

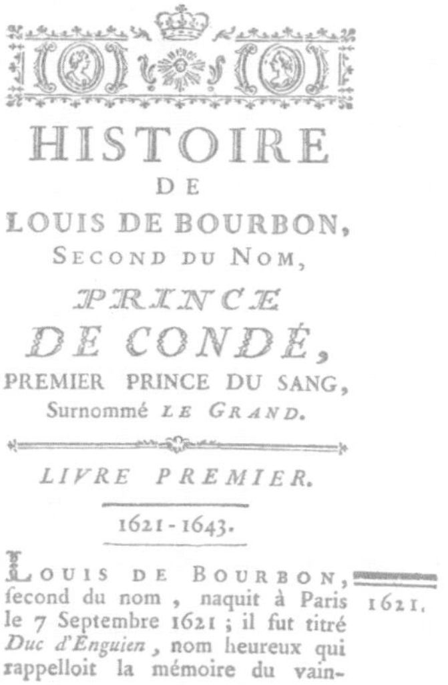

HISTOIRE
DE
LOUIS DE BOURBON,
SECOND DU NOM,

PRINCE
DE CONDÉ,
PREMIER PRINCE DU SANG,
Surnommé LE GRAND.

LIVRE PREMIER.

1621 - 1643.

LOUIS DE BOURBON, second du nom , naquit à Paris 1621. le 7 Septembre 1621 ; il fut titré Duc d'Enguien , nom heureux qui rappelloit la mémoire du vain-

Fig. 3

Opening page of Histoire de Louis de Bourbon *by Joseph-Louis Ripault Désormeaux, Paris, 1768. Typographic ornaments and letterforms by Pierre-Simon Fournier.*

William Pole
of Bally-Finn Esq.ʳ

Fig. 4

Rococo-styled engraved trade card of asymmetric design, c. 1770.

in a diminished, darker, heavier form – became a feature of Victorian design during the nineteenth century. Rococo was just one of several quite distinct styles whose popularity would rise and fall during this period in Britain. Many Victorian design styles assimilated by the printer came from international, historical models, such as the Arts and Crafts movement, whose roots were in the medieval tradition of craftsmanship. Similarly, when Japan opened its borders in 1853, the simplicity and purity of form of Japanese art was critically praised and led to 'Japanesque' typefaces such as Mikado being designed, as well as Japanese-themed ranges of typographic ornaments.

Fig. 5

Victorian book cover. Poetical Works of William Cowper, *George Routledge & Sons, London, 1900.*

As mentioned in the previous chapter, typographic ornaments were not always popular within the print trade, and this may in part explain why, during the late Georgian and Victorian periods, printers' flowers became larger to provide increased coverage with more ease and efficiency. Technical advances also helped to achieve this. The nature of the printing trade was also changing, with a greater proportion of printed matter now concerned with the commercial needs of manufacturing industries and mass production in general. However, within the book trade, printers' flowers, and more specifically classic arabesques, still remained in use, although generally applied with little thought or relish. Meanwhile, cover design became much more lively, especially from around 1880, as publishers began to discover the effect of ornament and colour on sales (fig. 5).

The most important twentieth-century figure in the revival of typographic ornament as an integral part of the book was the American designer Bruce Rogers (fig. 6). Although, like so many of his contemporaries, impressed by the books of William Morris's Kelmscott Press, Rogers did not emulate Morris's style, but instead took inspiration from the fifteenth-century Italian scholar-printers whose work had originally inspired Morris.

During the first decade of the twentieth century, Rogers increasingly used printers' flowers as an alternative to commissioning illustrations. The culmination of Rogers'

Fig. 6

Bruce Rogers, personal mark.

use of typographic ornament was, undoubtedly, the Grolier Club's *The Pierrot of the Minute*, designed in 1922 and published the following year (fig. 7). This book, decorated throughout with fragile garlands and moons, demonstrates Rogers' consummate ability to make printers' flowers transcend the practicalities of typesetting. But it was a hard-won triumph, requiring extensive trials and false starts, each page having to be hand-set by compositors, only to be repeatedly taken apart and reset as Rogers searched for a satisfactory solution.

Rogers' unorthodox way of working was to create his design by inking individual printers' flowers, using a stamp pad, and then impressing them on to paper.[6] It was from his elemental handmade design that the compositor would have to construct a practical solution using metal flowers – a demanding process, especially when the ornaments were arranged in arcs, curves and diagonals. Rogers' method required the very small individual flowers to be carefully filed and mitred with extreme accuracy to enable them to be securely locked into position in a metal frame that was then moved to the press. Nevertheless, by this process, he established the design of print as an activity closely aligned to, but quite separate from, the highest levels of printing craftsmanship. The designer of print – the 'graphic designer' – had, in everything but name, been established, and it was the complexity and the expressive potential afforded by typographic ornament that had played a crucial role.

Fig. 7

Bruce Rogers, title page,
The Pierrot of the Minute,
Grolier Club, New York, 1923.

01

02

03

04

05

06

07

08

09

10

11

12

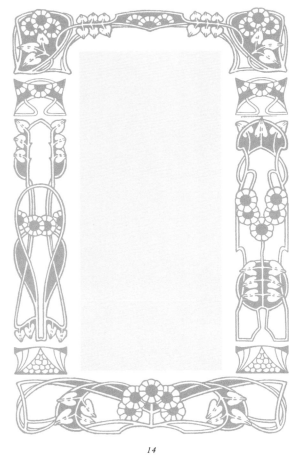

14

13

15

16

17

18

19

20

21

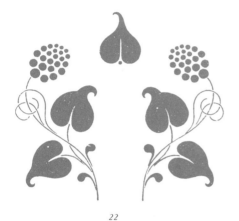

22

23

24

25

26

27

28

29

30

31

32

33

34

35

36

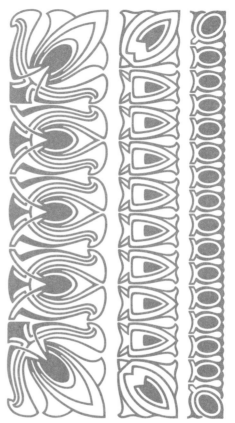

37

38

39

40

41

42

43

44

45

46

47

48

49

50

51

52

53

54

55

56

57

58

59

60

61

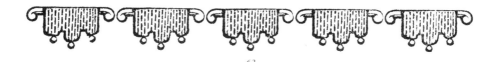

62

63

64

65

66

67

68

69

70

71

72

73

74

75

76

77

78

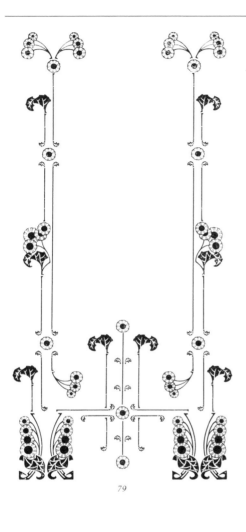

79

80

81

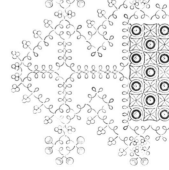

82

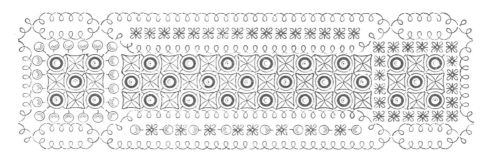

83

84

85

86

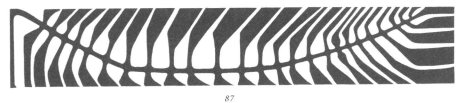

87

88

89

90

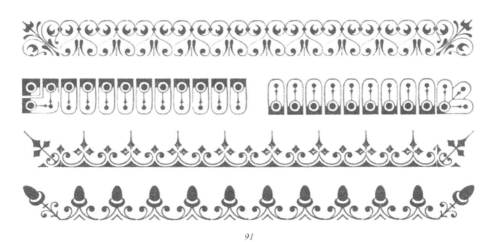

91

92

93

94

95

96

97

98

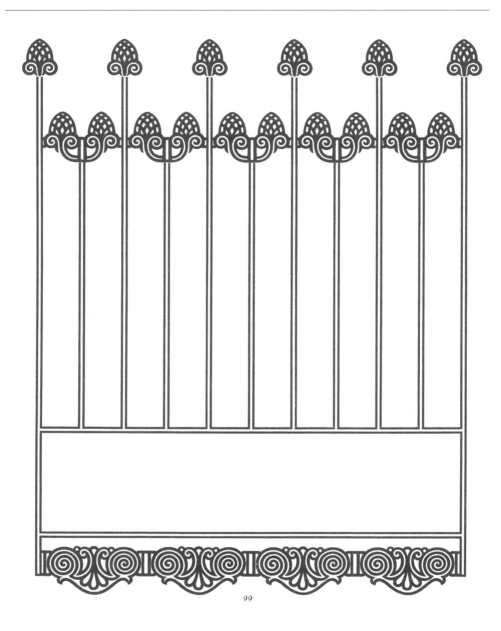

99

100

101

102

103

104

105

107

108

106

109

110

111

112

113

![decorative rectangular panel with floral motif]

114

![decorative swirl and floral borders]

115

116

117

118

119

120

121

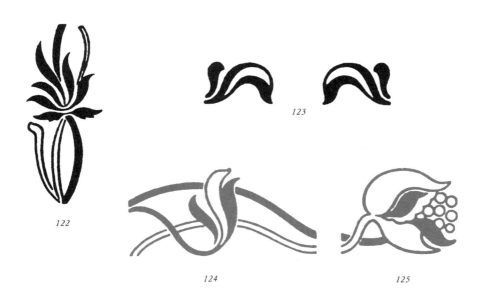

_122_

_123_

_124_

_125_

_126_

_127_

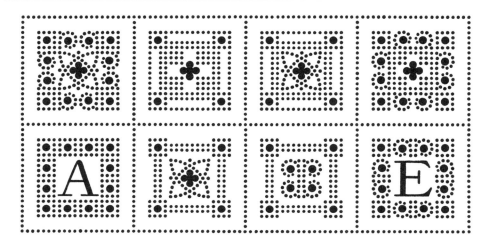

128

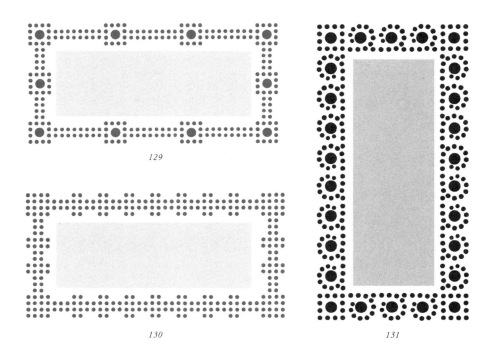

129

130

131

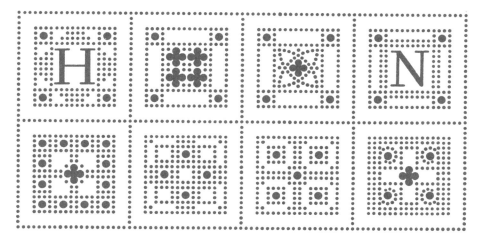

132

133

134

135

136

137

138

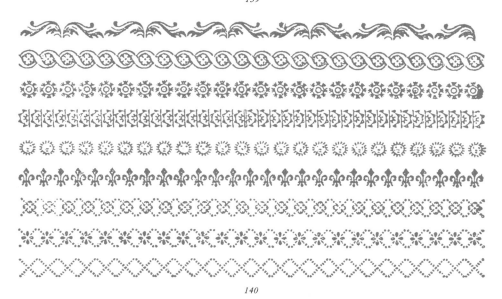

139

140

141

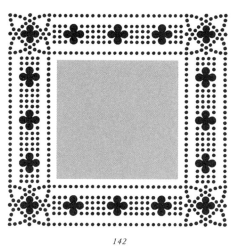

142

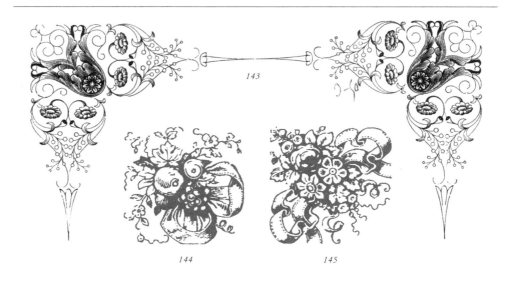

143

144   *145*

146

148

147

149

150

151

152

153

3
Geometric Ornamental Forms

In the aftermath of World War I, there was a dramatic change in both the appearance and use of typographic ornament. The overt complexity of the work produced in the final two decades of the nineteenth century, typified by the ornamental combination borders of the MacKellar, Smiths & Jordan type foundry in America (see Chapter 5), was now universally held in disdain. In Britain, the aesthetic values of the Victorian age – essentially historic in nature – were considered wholly inappropriate for a 'progressive' and fully industrialized world. Modernism promised a more open and honest, streamlined, equal and efficient society built by designers using man-made, mass-produced, cheap and renewable materials. The emphasis was to be wholly on the future

Fig. 2

Symbol for the Bauhaus Press, designed by László Moholy-Nagy, 1923.

rather than the past and the 'random clutter' of late nineteenth-century printing (fig. 1) – especially its dependence on ornament – was now despised by a new, culturally aware, more business-like generation of typographic designers.[7]

Another huge difference was that this new typographic style was designed specifically to meet the needs of a maturing advertising industry as well as to promote a growing service and manufacturing base. Its simplicity of form, often consisting of elemental squares, circles, triangles and portions thereof, was designed to support a new generation of bold, characterful sans serif types – also called, appropriately, 'geometric' types – which were ideal for adding emphasis or simply to catch the eye.

Since Modernism was concerned primarily with dismissing everything non-essential, it is surprising to find that typographic ornament – albeit in these new, more utilitarian forms – was hugely popular. Even more surprising, then, that its popularity was thanks largely to the influence of the Bauhaus – the epicentre of Modernist thinking – and in particular, the teacher and designer László Moholy-Nagy. Moholy-Nagy incorporated the square, circle and triangle ornaments into the design school's printed matter and used them as the symbol for the Bauhaus Press in 1923 (fig. 2). These elemental forms, which Moholy-Nagy described as the 'fundamental grammar of visual communication', were suddenly given prominence in German foundry specimen catalogues. The nature of international trade in foundry type ensured that British and European catalogues were soon seen in North America. The combination of simple shapes, often in conjunction with primary colours – another Bauhaus-led innovation – marked a conspicuous transformation in typographic ornaments.

These building blocks of visual grammar were soon taken up by designers and compositors alike, who used them to construct images – something the foundries encouraged in their promotional material (fig. 3). The shapes were even used in the design of letterforms (fig. 4) rather than simply as decorative material, as initially intended. The simplicity of these images follows the edict 'Less is more', meaning that all superfluous information was, by default, edited out to leave what could be described as the 'essence' of the issue in hand. For the Bauhaus this process was about rationality, functionality and a new objectivity. Away from the Bauhaus, in trade printers' workshops, advertising art studios and design consultancies, the potential for a more playful use of these building blocks was explored.

Making images from typographic ornaments was not new – Bruce Rogers in America provided many such examples (fig. 5) – but the new, purely geometric ornaments encouraged a very different, more overt and entertaining use. Albert Schiller, art director of the Advertising Agencies' Service in New York, was a leading exponent of the style and had an exhibition of his work (fig. 6) at the New York Public Library in 1952 titled 'Machine-Age Art' (see p. 233).

Fig. 3

Elementare
Schmuckformen,
*or 'Elementary Decorative
Forms' specimen booklet,
D. Stempel AG, Frankfurt
am Main, 1927.*

EUCLID

A NEW TYPE

Fig. 4

*Alvin Lustig, Euclid,
a new type designed from
typographic ornaments, late
1930s. This experimental
typeface led to the design for
the masthead of the* Arts and
Architecture *magazine.*

It was more likely to be designers, such as Schiller, rather than compositors, who were using geometric typographic ornaments, if only because of the designer's more inventive nature. As designers became more influential, type foundries adjusted the way they presented their fonts and typographic ornaments in their specimen books by displaying them in the form of simulated adverts, and using a language aimed at the designer. The German foundry D. Stempel AG explained in its type specimen catalogue *Elementare Schmuckformen* ('Elementary Decorative Forms') of 1927: 'Elementary geometric shapes offer virtually unlimited creative possibilities for the imaginative design of print.'

A renewed interest in traditional craftsmanship was encouraging a new and refreshing attitude to typographic ornament in Britain in the 1910s. At the forefront was the typographer Francis Meynell, first at Burns & Oates and then at his own Pelican Press. His enthusiasm was to influence his friend and colleague Stanley Morison, who as typographic advisor to the Monotype Corporation set in motion the re-cutting and production of many traditional typographic ornaments. Meynell's work also influenced Oliver Simon at the Curwen Press (renowned for its formidable printing standards harnessed to intelligent design), where a new and outstanding generation of artists was commissioned to design typographic ornaments, some of which were unstintingly geometric in style (fig. 7).

In America during the 1910s, William A. Dwiggins, type designer, book designer and calligrapher, and famously the first to describe his activity as 'graphic design', was also a devoted craftsman who relished exploring ways of bypassing mechanical processes wherever possible.[8] Typical of this approach were his many and varied hand-cut stencil designs of ornaments made using celluloid. He found using stencils cut with a knife provided him with a sharper, more uniform result than pen and ink or brushwork and harmonized better with the crispness of printed letterforms. These small ornaments, often a hybrid mix of

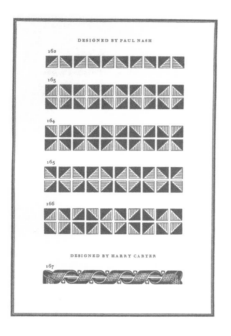

Fig. 7

*Geometric typographic
ornaments designed by
Paul Nash for the Curwen
Press, c. 1935.*

Fig. 8

*William A. Dwiggins,
typographic ornaments made
from hand-cut stencils, 1930s.*

geometric and organic forms (it is impossible to categorize *anything* Dwiggins did), would be multiplied for dramatic effect and used to visualize and build up decorative requirements such as borders, headpieces and endpaper patterns. Dwiggins also very successfully extended his use of ornaments to illustration work (fig 8). While many designers emulated Bruce Rogers, no one could come near Dwiggins for his liberated and entirely unique approach to typographic ornament.

With the hounding and eventual closure of the Bauhaus in Germany in 1933, geometric ornamental forms took on a different and, encouraged by Albert Schiller, rather more exploratory aspect. This is the subject of Chapter 7: Ingenious Art.

154

155

156

157

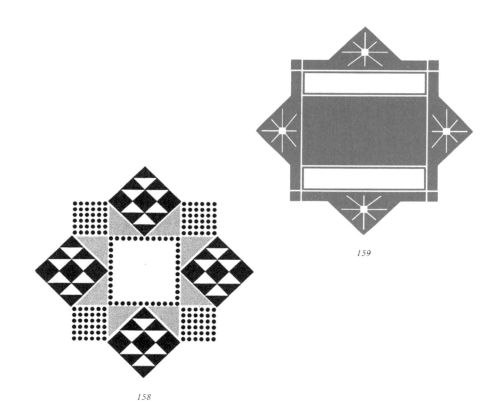

159

158

160

161

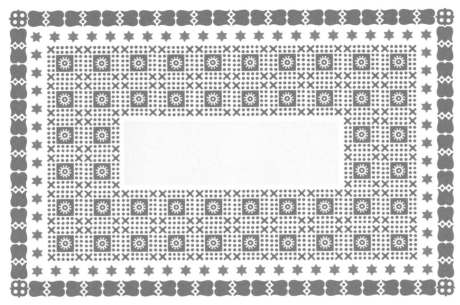

162

163

164

165

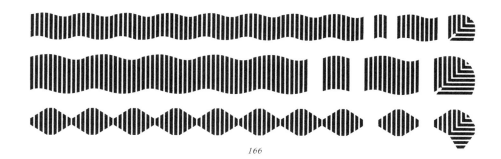

166

167

168

169

170

171

172

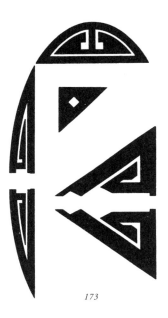

173

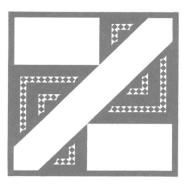

174

175

176

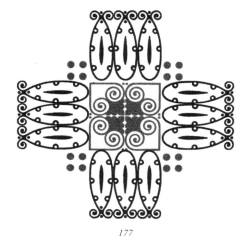

177

178

179

180

181

182

183

184

185

186

187

188

189

190

191

192

193

194

195

196

197

198

199

200

201

202

203

204

205

206

207

208

209

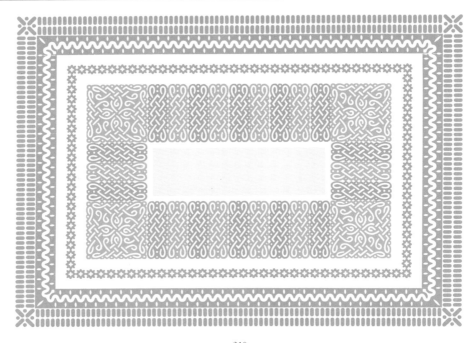

210

211

212

213

214

215

216

217

218

219

220

221

222

223

224

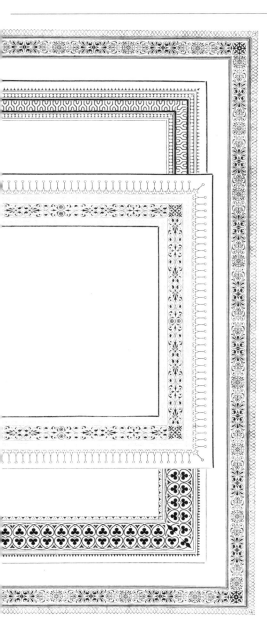

225

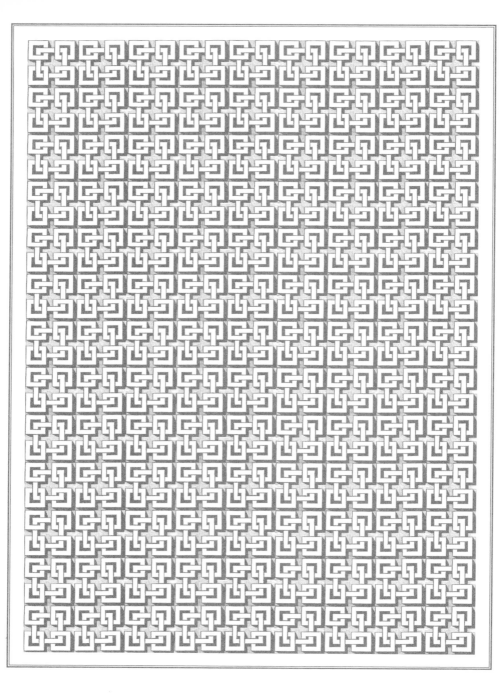

4
Ornamental Rules
& Borders

It had long been thought that typographic ornament was the most quixotic aspect of the compositor's craft. However, its use was, arguably, made even more demanding by Pierre-Simon Fournier in the mid eighteenth century when, by eschewing the more formal arabesque designs of the previous century, he created new ornaments that could be used as single units of decoration *or* in multiple combinations, to form vignettes or borders. In other words, the design of Fournier's flowers did not dictate, or even hint at, how they should be arranged or used in the composition of borders, or indeed anything else. This was an unfamiliar prospect for a compositor used to working within clearly defined standard rules, but it offered an unprecedented level of freedom, limited only by the compositor's imagination.

Fig. 1

Pierre-Simon Fournier, title page of his Modèles des Caractères, *Paris, 1742.*

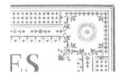

Fig. 2

Pierre-Simon Fournier, detail from the title page pictured above in Fig. 1. Note the mitred corners of the heavy rules.

Fournier himself described the setting of ornaments as being 'the [most] difficult and artistic parts of the book'. But of all the functions to which printers' flowers were put, setting a border was probably the most common and also the most daunting. For this reason, many larger printer-publishers employed a compositor who specialized in the setting of typographic ornaments.

A border is a repeated decorative design. This might simply be a plain rule with mitred corners, or a pattern effectively cast on to a rule of whatever length (see p. 8). It can be (and more often is) made up of multiples of individual units turned through 90 or 180 degrees to create repeated patterns. The complexity of such a design depends entirely on the designer's personal inclination, the time available and the appropriateness of the subject in hand. However, it is inconceivable that a tour de force such as Fournier's type specimen book *Modèles des Caractères*, 1742 (fig. 1), could be recreated by an effort of the imagination alone. A designer using Fournier's flowers would need to have access to the actual physical units, or at least printed proofs, in order to understand and fully appreciate the endless possibilities and creative opportunities they offered.

In addition, Fournier's remarkable technical skill enabled him to extend the repertoire of typographic ornaments. For example, his explorations into casting enabled him to cast single-, double- and triple-ruled lines and to offer the largest metal type available (amazingly, equivalent to contemporary 84- and 108-point sizes).[9] Significantly, Fournier never regarded his typographic ornaments as an afterthought, but instead as an essential complement to his new types. Some border ornaments could be arranged to form a pale-textured ground over which a bolder design could be printed, while others were near-pictorial items, suggesting sunbursts (fig. 2), medallions and garlands. With Fournier's ornaments to hand, used alongside his floriated and script types, or *lettres de fantaisie*, the

compositor could design decorative borders to match the celebrated freedom and virtuosity of the engraver (fig. 3).

Fournier's typographic ornaments were admired more than they were used during the nineteenth century. Simpler ornamental borders, exemplified by those of Giambattista Bodoni, quickly overshadowed the complexity of Fournier's work and dominated the 1800s. It was not until the twentieth century, thanks largely to the influence of Bruce Rogers in North America and Francis Meynell in England, that Fournier's ornaments began to enjoy a resurgence of interest.

Between 1900, when the Monotype Corporation in the UK issued its first typeface, and 1922, when Stanley Morison was appointed its typographic advisor, Monotype's typographic ornaments consisted largely of the geometric shapes so popular at that time. In the few years that followed, mainly in response to the renewed vogue for printers' flowers led by the work of Meynell, the number of arabesques it produced increased substantially. The following year, Meynell, together with Morison, wrote 'Printers' Flowers and Arabesques' for the first issue of *The Fleuron.* Under Morison's direction, Monotype undertook a unique and ambitious programme of research and re-cutting of historic typefaces and typographic ornaments. Significantly,

Fig. 4

Typographic ornaments that accompanied the typeface Fournier, released by Monotype in 1924.

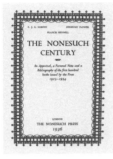

Fig. 5

Francis Meynell, title page of
The Nonesuch Century,
London, 1936.

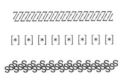

Fig. 6

*Simple borders created by the
author with standard letters
and numerals.*

one of the corporation's first revisions was of the typeface Fournier, which was released in 1924 and complemented by numerous ornaments from the same original source (fig. 4).[10] Single-handedly, Morison re-established the concept of ornamental rules and borders as an intrinsic element in the printer's repertoire.

There followed a spectacular display of Monotype's typographic ornaments a few years later in 1928 as *Printers Ornaments Applied to the Composition of Decorative Borders, Panels and Patterns.* The work, designed by the American Frederic Warde, was commissioned to demonstrate, as well as promote, Monotype's impressive range of typographic ornaments and, in particular, their magnificent use as borders. It is testimony to Warde that one of these border designs was closely replicated by Meynell for the title page of *The Nonesuch Century* some eight years later (fig. 5).

The design of Meynell's title page demonstrated how, with imagination and a little technical invention, decorative borders could be strikingly individual. For although Meynell's border included several standard printers' flowers, it also used 36 standard parentheses as decoration and achieved its distinctive 'portcullis' effect by the simple use of a 'multiple' rule cut into 256 short pieces.[11] Meynell's playful approach to ornamental border design proved the potential of 'standard' characters in the creation of decorative rules (fig. 6).

The 1920s was indeed a golden period for typographic ornament, and it was during this decade that the Curwen Press in London, renowned for its distinctive use of ornament, would establish itself (fig. 7). Oliver Simon, acting as art director, and company director Harold Curwen commissioned work from, among others, Edward Bawden, Eric Ravilious (fig. 8), Barnett Freedman and Paul Nash, all of whom designed ornamental material in the form of printers' flowers, decorative borders and pattern papers. Thanks largely to Simon, Curwen's use of typographic ornament – and borders in particular – caused a major resurgence in their popularity within

the British printing trade, and also in the USA, between 1920 and the beginning of the Second World War in 1939.[12]

For Simon and Curwen, good typography would always be efficient, simple and distinctive, yet they did not consider the non-essential to be necessarily superfluous. The idea that Curwen presswork should sparkle – be uplifting – was considered fundamental to its purpose. Typographic rules and borders, as used by the Curwen Press, had less to do with attraction, and rather more to do with avoiding what Simon called 'the designer gesture'. For them, the rich heritage represented by printers' flowers offered an attractive but suitably hushed support to the text. Common to all Curwen Press work is the link Simon achieved between the best of the printer's traditional craft – discussed here in the use of decorative borders and vignettes – with present-day printing technology.

226

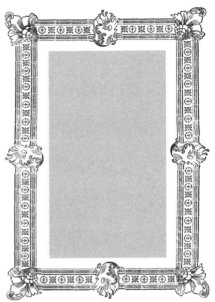

227

228

229

230

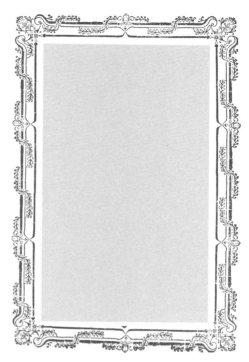

231

232

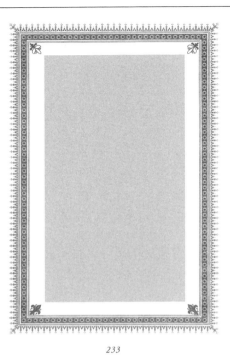

233

235

234

236

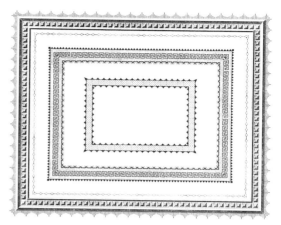

237

238

239

240

241

242

243

244

245

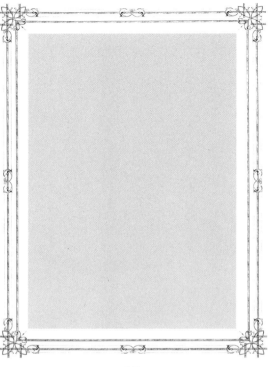

246

247

248

249

250

251

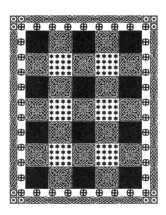

252

253

254

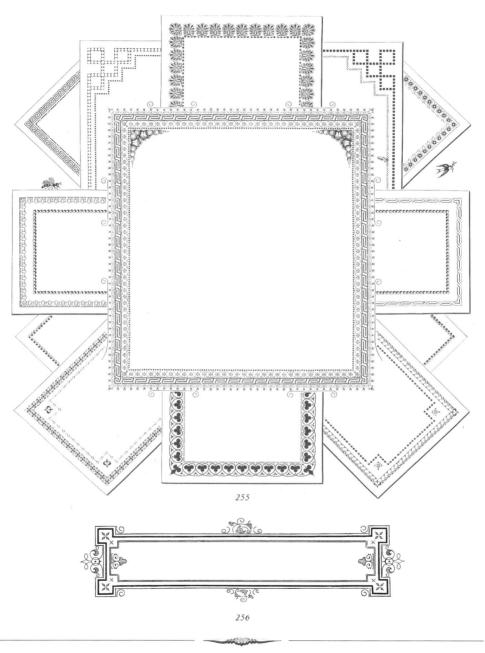

255

256

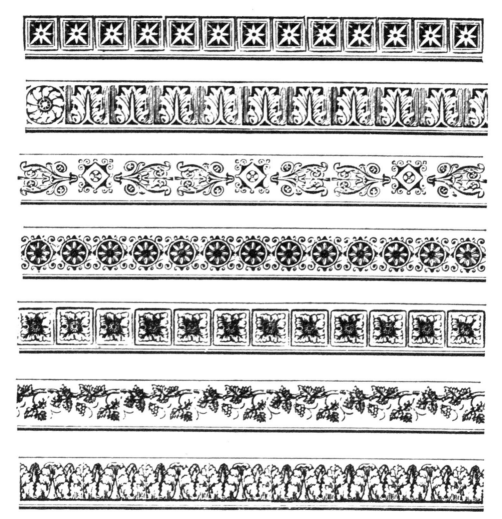

257

258

259

260

261

262

263

264

265

266

267

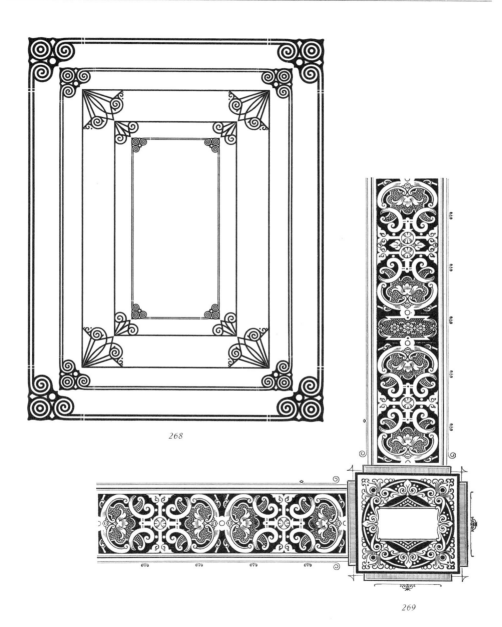

268

269

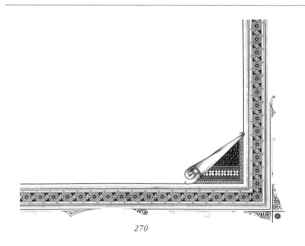

270

271

272

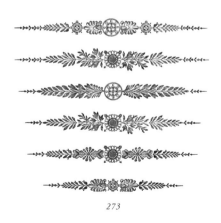

273

274

275

276

277

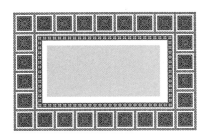

278

279

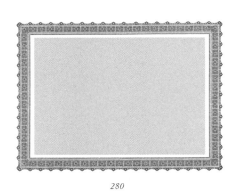

280

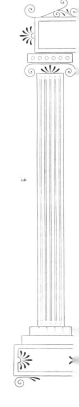

281

282

283

284

285

286

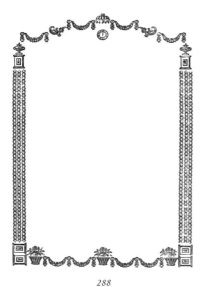

288

287

289

290

291

292

293

294

295

296

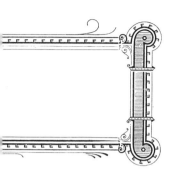

297

298

299

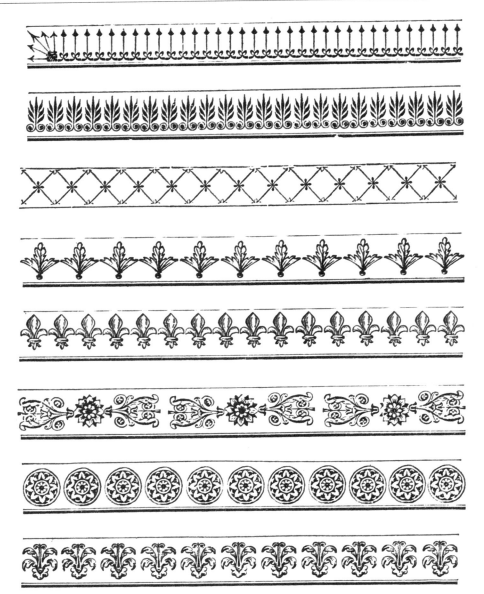

300

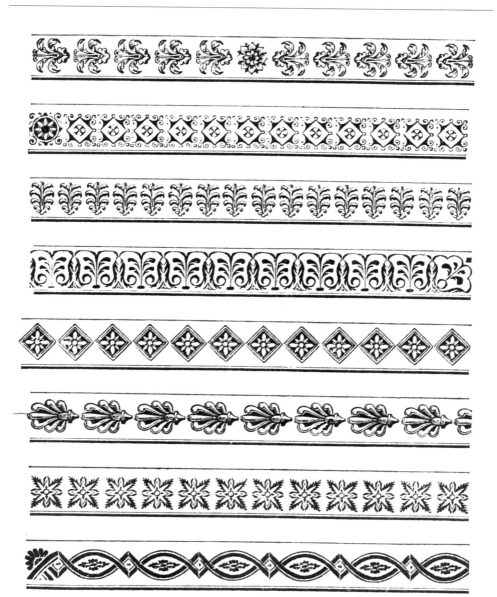

301

302

303

304

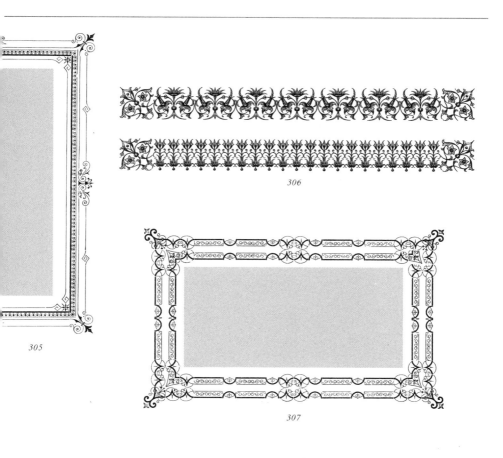

305

306

307

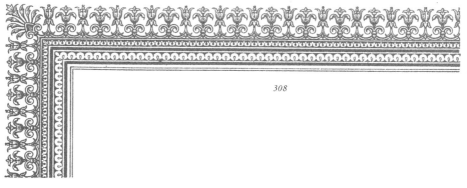

308

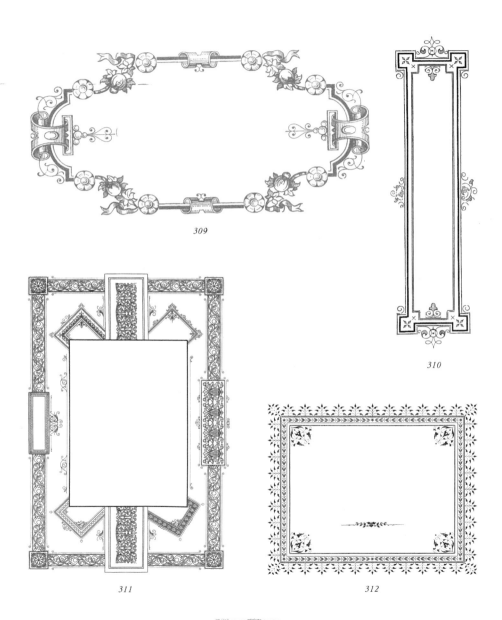

309

310

311

312

313

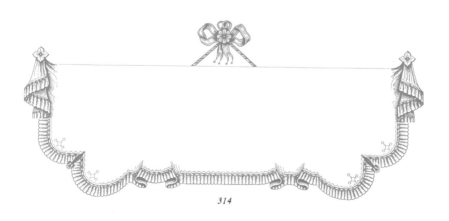

314

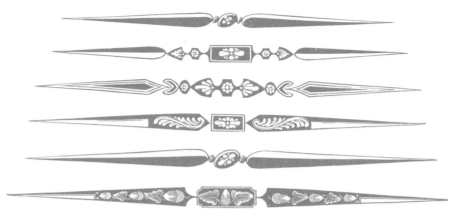

315

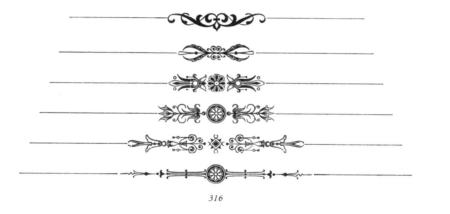

316

317

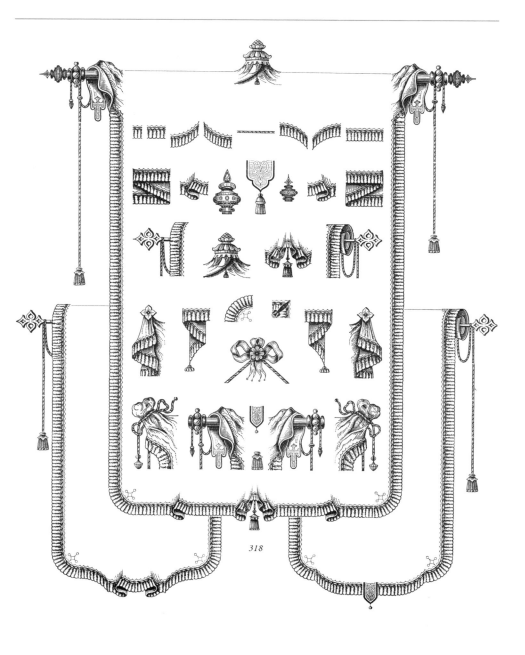

318

319

320

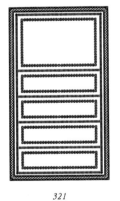

321

322

323

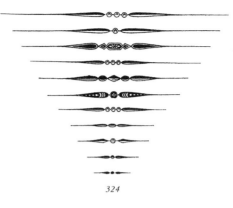

324

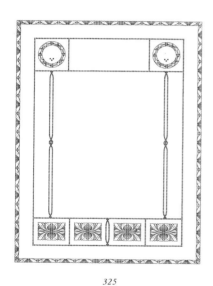

325

326

327

328

329

330

331

332

333

334

335

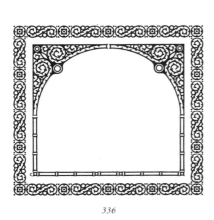

336

337

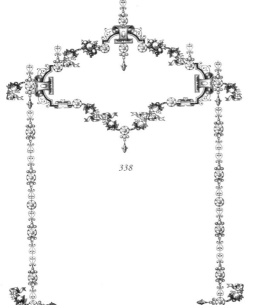

338

339

340

341

342

343

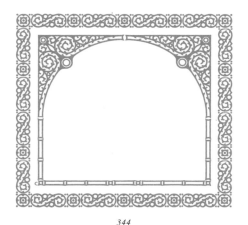

344

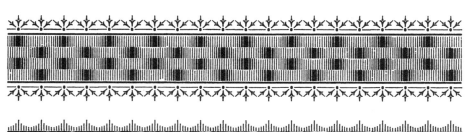

345

346

347

348

5
Combination Borders, Wreaths & Scrolls

Aware of the technical limitations of compositors (to say nothing of the additional time required to compose typographic ornaments), the major international type foundries began, from around the middle of the nineteenth century, to design and manufacture ready-made one-piece typographic ornamental solutions to solve many of the generic design problems. For example, wreaths – effectively typographic ornaments in the form of a circle or oval – were now sold as a single block with a space in the centre in which the printer could place the required words. Scrolls offered a similar 'stock' solution, providing commonly used words such as 'and', 'to' and 'office of', in various formulations, using decorative or cursive lettering often with an elaborate array of swashes. The words 'Bought of' (meaning 'bought from' and often shortened to 'Bot' or 'Bt. of') were a common expression, as was 'Dr. to' (meaning 'debtor to') (fig. 1). Both continued to be used in Britain, Europe and America until the 1950s.

Such ready-made artwork was produced using a process called stereotyping. This enabled an original engraved design (a decorative pattern, image, word or any combination of these) to be duplicated quickly and very cheaply. Making a stereotype consisted of two stages. The first required a mould to be made by pressing a layer of papier mâché on to the (usually wooden) hand-engraved image or hand-set typographic ornaments to be copied. Once the mould had dried, the second stage involved casting a copy from the mould using molten type metal. The resulting 'stereo', usually about 4 mm (⅙ in) thick, was then mounted on to a wood block and planed to the same height as the metal type.[13] The result was called a 'stock block' or, in the USA, a 'stock cut'. Later, in the 1920s, stereos would be made curved so that they could be used on the much faster rotary presses, and papier-mâché moulds would be replaced by plastic or rubber ones.

Stereotyping not only made decorative and pictorial images, combination borders and wreaths far easier to use, but also made them cheap and easy to buy. It is not surprising, then, that during the second half of the nineteenth century there was a huge proliferation in the use of illustrations and typographic ornament, especially in advertising, packaging, trade catalogues and magazines (fig. 2). The ability

Fig. 1

Page from the Thorowgood type foundry catalogue displaying a range of 'Bought of' cast ornaments, London, c. 1880s.

to make unlimited copies of a design meant that small items such as tickets or calling cards could be printed in multiples of four, six or more to a sheet, while larger items could be printed simultaneously on several presses. As the scale of manufacturing around the world increased, printed advertising became national – and even international – in scope and stereotyping played its part by enabling advertisements to be organized and distributed so that they could appear simultaneously in an unlimited number of publications.

This was also the period in which American type foundries really came to the fore. One of the most influential of these (as we have seen) was MacKellar, Smiths & Jordan based in Philadelphia, a major centre for printing and publishing. The company was established in 1796, but it was not until 1860, with a change of ownership, that it became one of the world's most innovative makers of display typefaces and typographic ornaments.

It was during the 1880s that MacKellar, Smiths & Jordan introduced typefaces with decorative backgrounds. When set side-by-side into words, the letters combined to provide the effect of a continuous pattern running behind

the type. In this way, typefaces such as Arboret (1884) and
Arboret 2 (1885) ingeniously blurred word and image, letters and ornament, into one. As well as the decorative
background, Arboret also incorporated a line above and
below the typeface which, when set, connected perfectly.
End-stops or 'caps' were provided to be set at the beginning
and end of the word to complete the image of a panel (fig.
3). An earlier typeface, Relievo (1878), although technically
less innovative, provided the effective illusion of the letters
bursting out of the panel (fig. 4). Such *trompe l'oeil* effects
gave the letterpress printer the means to compete with the
technical freedom of the signwriter (who was able to paint
letters on shop fronts in any size, colour or style) and the
burgeoning lithographic printer who, during the nineteenth
century, had very effectively replaced the engraver as the
letterpress printer's main competitor (figs 5a and b).

These 'combination' sets provided a degree of flexibility to the letterpress printer that became translated by
its enthusiasts into artistic endeavour. Indeed, a movement
calling itself Artistic Printing became an established force
within the jobbing printing fraternity in America from
around 1879. Equally enthusiastic practitioners in the UK
quickly followed suit and, in a bid to revitalize a lacklustre
job printing industry, established *The Printers' International
Specimen Exchange* in 1880 (fig. 6). Edited by Andrew White

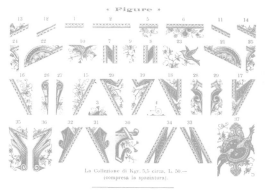

NEBIOLO & COMP., TORINO

Fig. 5a

Thirty-seven Zig-Zag border units, designed and manufactured by MacKellar, Smiths & Jordan, 1880. This page is from the catalogue of an Italian foundry, one of many companies around the world acting as distributors for MSJ products.

Fig. 5b

A sample demonstration of how Zig-Zag border units might be used. From the catalogue of MacKellar, Smiths & Jordan, c. 1880.

Tuer (co-proprietor of Field & Tuer and its publishing imprint, the Leadenhall Press), this annual publication aimed to encourage and nurture an ambitious, more artistic approach in the composing room. The *Exchange* contained almost exclusively jobbing work, much of it with typographic ornament to the fore, and included examples from across Europe and the USA as well as the UK.

This was a period when, quite suddenly, names of individual compositors as well as companies became common appendages to printed matter. Recognition of the compositor's efforts in this way represented an entirely new attitude

within a printing industry where self-effacement and equality of status within and across all its activities had been considered more appropriate. Perhaps it was, in part, the intention to impress, or at least draw attention, that caused the new 'artistic printers' to use increasing amounts of decorative material and the most extrovert of display fonts to create work of unrivalled complexity (fig. 7).

The scale of MacKellar, Smiths & Jordan as a company, (see p. 13, fig. 8), together with its early expertise in stereotyping, meant that it could eventually offer one of the larger collections of stock blocks and ornaments in America – at its height totalling about 5,000 different 'images'. These included sundry items such as date lines and cheque blanks (commonly used in nineteenth-century financial transactions), calling cards and billhead logotypes, state seals, national and society emblems, as well as a multitude of blocks illustrating every kind of trade. However, although the quantity may be impressive, many of these stock blocks were not unique to MacKellar, Smiths & Jordan. It was only after the success of its typeface Relievo that the company became renowned for its own patented combination border series, the first, in 1879, offering a Japanese theme.

It was possibly the success of illusionistic typefaces such as Relievo and Arboret that encouraged the company

Fig. 7

Trade card for an ink manufacturer, designed and printed by Haight & Dudley, New York, c. 1880.

to develop the concept of 'combination border series'. Although this was not, in itself, a new concept, MacKellar, Smiths & Jordan's combination borders took the idea of blending word and image to an ingenious and technically more sophisticated level. Each series consisted of perhaps thirty or more small, thematically designed cast images (such as storks, dragonflies, boats, human figures and other individual images) that could be seamlessly composed together with units designed to form decorative rules, borders or panels. Composed in this way, a scene depicting, for example, a Japanese interior and landscape could be created (fig. 8).

Other combination border series followed, incorporating popular exotic themes such as Egyptian, Asian and Chinese, and although MacKellar, Smiths & Jordan did not produce any more of these series after 1881, the border series continued to appear in its specimen books well into the 1890s.[14] The commercial success of combination borders caused a flurry of similar designs to be offered by other foundries, the most notable being the Bruce Type Foundry in New York and Schelter & Giesecke in Leipzig.

Fig. 8

Trade card for a jeweller, letterpress printed using the MacKellar, Smiths & Jordan Egyptian combination border series, 1883.

349

350

351

352

353

354

355

356

357

MAYEUR

358

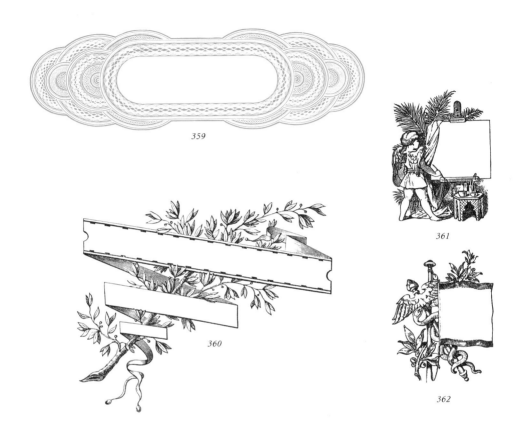

359

360

361

362

363

364

365

366

367

368

369

370

372

371

373

374

375

376

377

378

379

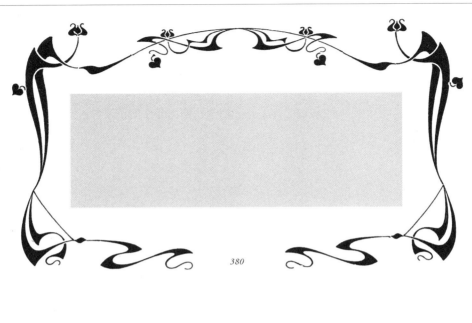

380

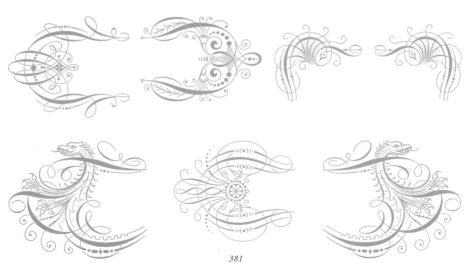

381

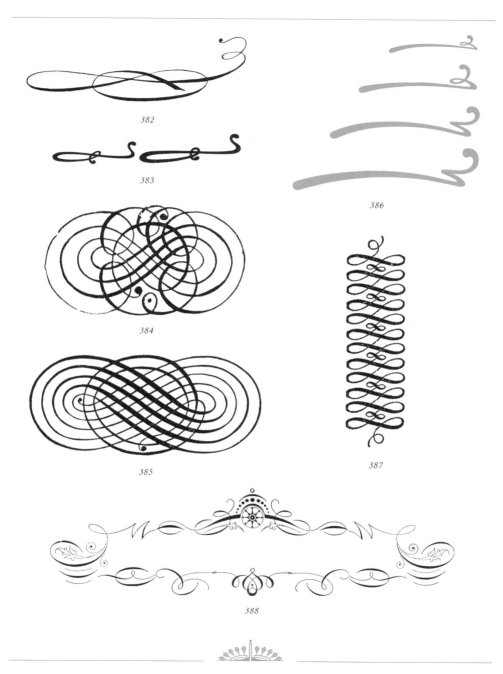

382

383

386

384

387

385

388

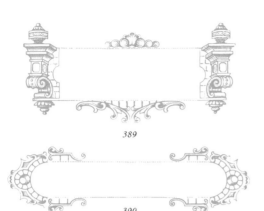

389

390

391

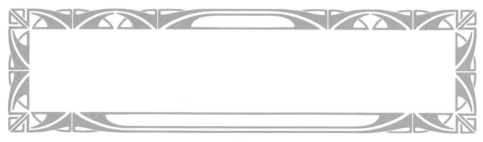

392

393

394

395

396

397

398

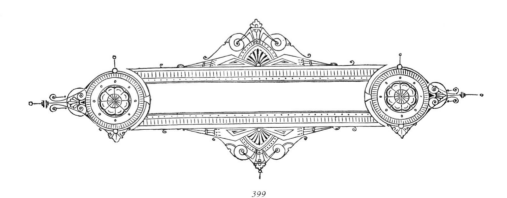

399

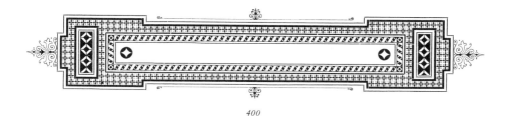

400

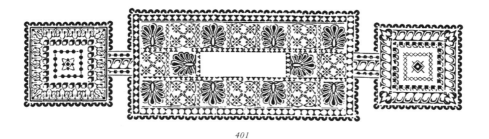

401

402

403

404

405

406

407

408

409

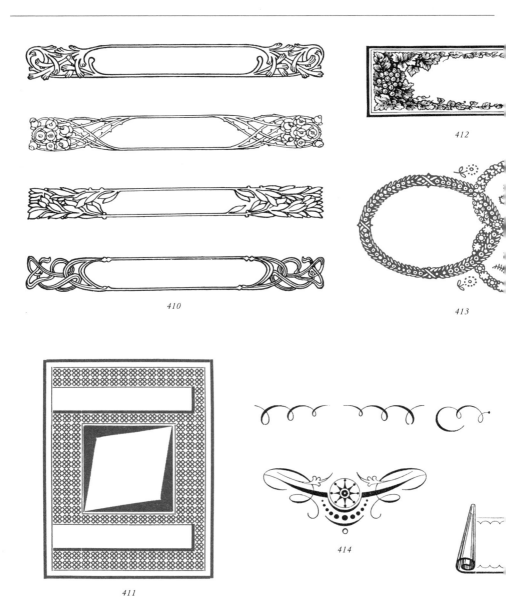

410

411

412

413

414

415

416

417

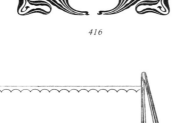

418

419

420

421

422

423

424

425

426

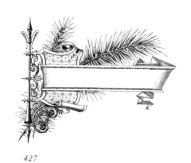

427

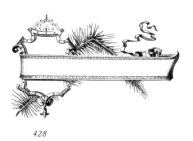

428

429

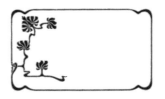

430

431

432

434

433

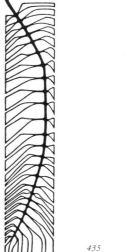

435

436

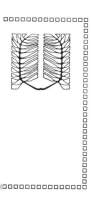

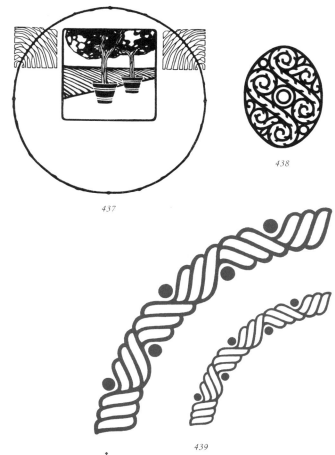

437

438

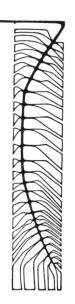

439

440

441

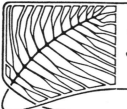

442

Scena Illustra
Giornale Mensile

443

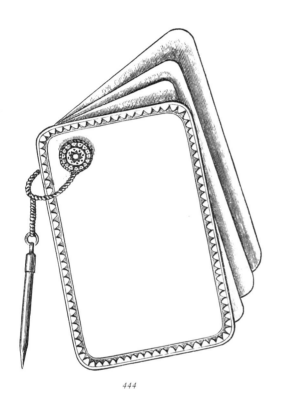

444

445

446

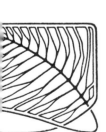

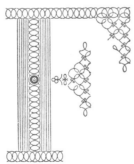 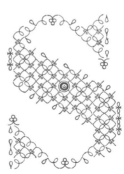

447

448

449

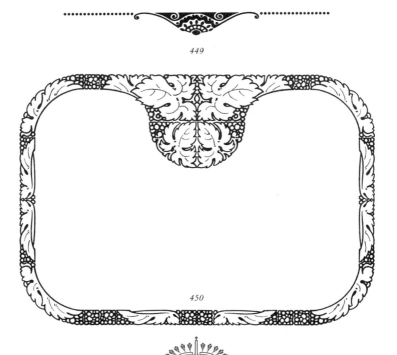

450

451

452

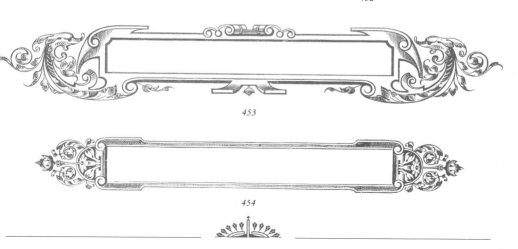

453

454

455

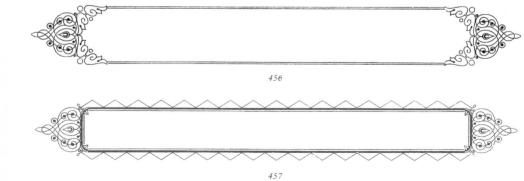

456

457

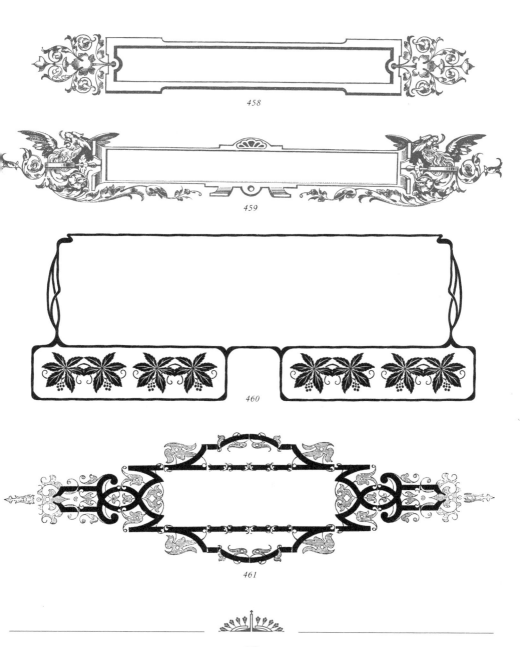

458

459

460

461

462

464

463

465

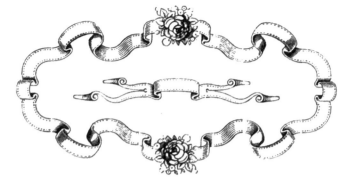

466

467

468

469

470

471

472

473

474

475

476

477

478

479

480

481

482

483

484

485

486

487

488

489

490

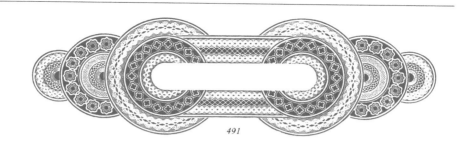

491

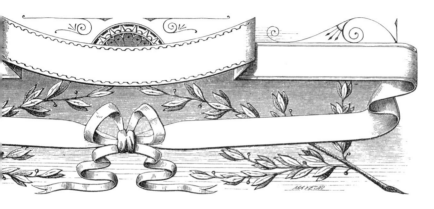

492

493

494

495

496

497

498

499

500

501

502

503

504

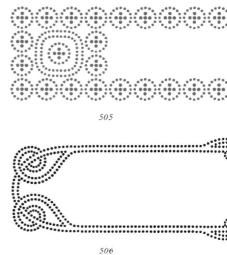

505

506

508

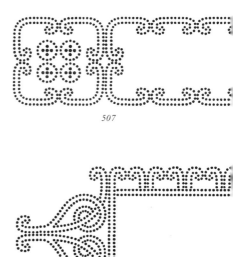

507

509

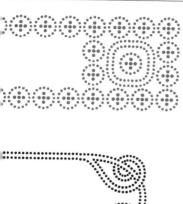

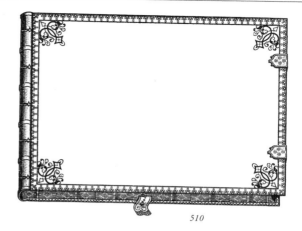

510

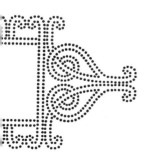

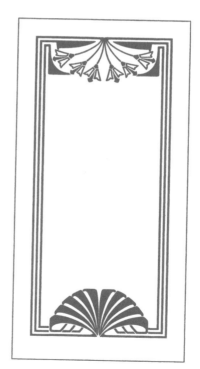

511

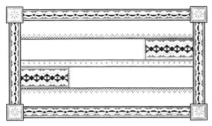

512

513

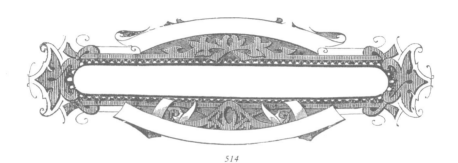

514

515

SECRET SOCIETIES

DIED.

MASONIC.

I.O.O.F.

BORN

Telegraphic.

MARRIED

THE FARM.

MUSIC AND THE DRAMA

POLITICAL.

HOME

POETRY.

RELIGIOUS NEWS.

MASONIC.

HUMOROUS.

AGRICULTURA

516

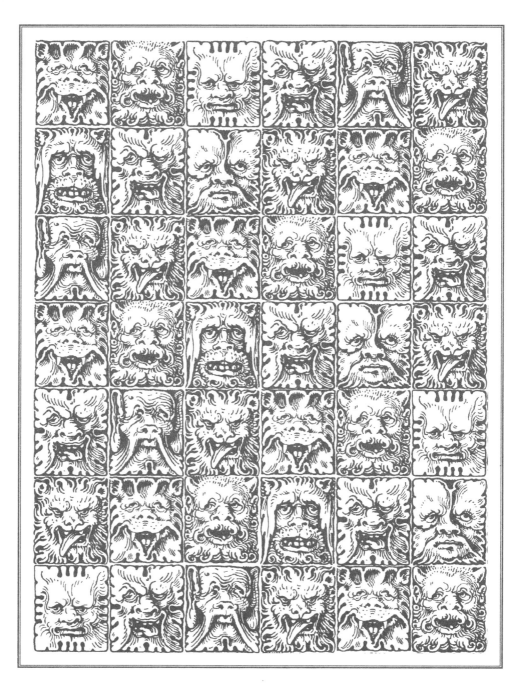

6
Pictorial
Ornaments

The commercial advantage of a picture being able to attract attention far more effectively than words was the reason for the high number of specialist engravers working in every major city of the developed world since the fifteenth century. However, the process of cutting a metal plate or a block of wood was slow, and so pictures were considered something of a luxury. The invention of stereotyping (see previous chapter) virtually revolutionized the appearance of print, enabling every printer to buy his own stock of images in anticipation of common printing commissions such as weddings and funerals, sporting events and regular trade. These stereotyped, mass-produced images were, therefore, commonly called 'stock blocks' or, in the USA, 'stock cuts'.

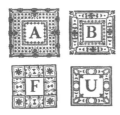

Stock blocks are generally accepted to have their origin in the large pictorial initial used to mark the opening of a passage of text, dating back to handwritten manuscripts, but still in common usage long after the invention of printing. Often hand-cut in wood, these were known as *factotums*, meaning 'general purpose', and usually had a space in the centre to take the first letter of the opening word of the passage (fig. 1). Because *factotums* were utilized in a broad range of printed material, from newspapers to formal legal documents, they were some of the earliest items to be stereotyped and made into blocks. As such, they remained in use well into the nineteenth century and beyond.

Stock blocks are considered to be ornaments because printers bought them from type foundries for general purpose – to be used and reused on a range of projects rather than for a single, specific exercise (fig. 2). For example, a stock block of a bull would be used to illustrate advertisements, posters and handbills for country fairs, as well as for cattle auctions or the high-street butcher.

Stock blocks were also used for the pictorial 'slug', introduced by Benjamin Franklin's *Pennsylvania Gazette* to act as a visual index in the small-advertisement columns (fig. 3). These small images occupied a depth of perhaps three or four lines of text and depicted popular topics such as transport (sailing ships, stagecoaches, and later trains and steamships) and agriculture (farm animals and tools) (fig. 4).

Initially, only engravers could supply printers with illustrative images, in the form of an engraved or 'cut' wood block. That was until type foundries began to mass-produce images as metal blocks through the process of stereotyping (see p. 142). By the end of the eighteenth century, many type foundries displayed a range of stock blocks in their specimen books (fig. 5). As the nineteenth century progressed, the volume and range of subject matter – together with the actual physical size of stock images – grew immensely, providing the jobbing letterpress printer with all he needed to illustrate his customer's billheads, handbills, posters and general

Fig. 3

Small newspaper notice advertising for passengers or merchants wishing to transport freight to New York, New York Herald, *c. 1835.*

Fig. 4

Page of small stock blocks, 'farm animals', Fonderie S. Berthier & Durey, Paris, 1890.

ephemera. Stock images were copied with impunity, a process aided by the invention of photography in around 1839.

By the mid nineteenth century, trade catalogues – illustrated with pictorial ornaments – had become a common way for manufacturers and retailers to advertise their wares. The first true modern trade catalogues were produced in England in about the 1760s with the specific purpose of selling goods produced by brass-founding and Sheffield plate manufacturers. Other manufacturing areas quickly began publishing their own catalogues, profusely illustrated with

Fig. 5

*Stock illustration, Ferdinand
Theinhardt type foundry,
Berlin, 1892.*

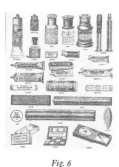

Fig. 6

*Page from a catalogue of
printing products, London, late
nineteenth century.*

clear and detailed engraved images of furniture, jewellery, glass, luxury clothing and domestic appliances as well as specialist product ranges for industries such as printing and design (fig. 6). Large department stores followed suit, with Harrods and the Army & Navy Co-operative Society in the UK, Montgomery Ward & Co. in the USA, and Les Grands Magasins du Louvre, Au Bon Marché and Printemps in France all producing their own catalogues.

The commercial function of a changing image on the cover of a journal or catalogue was well understood, and the harnessing of photography to this end was something that printers recognized had huge economic potential. News magazines such as *The Illustrated London News* (fig. 7) were often printed with a single large wood-engraved cover illustration, but such a major commission could take five or more days to complete, making a speedy response to a breaking news story impractical.

Then, in around 1860, photographic technology revolutionized the activity of the engraver and the manufacture of stock blocks.[15] A method was discovered of sensitizing the surface of wood to enable a photographic image to be exposed on to it.[16] This breakthrough provided the engraver with an image, complete with detail and tones, transferred directly on to the surface of the wood. The engraver could then create a relief image by cutting through the photograph into the wood block. Equally important was the fact that such photographic images, despite the interpretive role of the engraver, had sufficient cachet for other news-based publications to pay for a copy of the image in the form of a stereo. The result was that multiple-copied stereotyped wood-engraved images depicting people or events of international significance became highly profitable and helped to establish the status of the photographer, often to the detriment of the engraver.

The scale of production and the variety of stereotypes (later superseded and made easier by the electrotype process) was enormous. For example, the Franklin Engraving and Electroplating Company in Chicago, established in 1880 – one of many that specialized in stereotypes – had a catalogue of almost 10,000 decorative stock illustrations. Customers were also encouraged to come up with ideas for images of their own, which were sketched for approval before being engraved.

The art of engraving went into decline once it was realized that a pen-and-ink drawing could also be photographed and transferred to a wood block coated with a light-sensitive solution (fig. 8). It quickly followed that the same photographic image could be transferred to a metal plate but this time coated with a solution that hardened in contact with light and acted as a resist when the plate was placed in acid. This process, developed in about the 1840s, came to be known as photo-engraving, and was generally done by small, specialist enterprises to service jobbing printers. Meanwhile, large printing companies (especially those involved in newspaper and magazine publishing) quickly realized the benefits of having image-processing departments of their own, both for economic and security reasons.

The growth of illustration used in newspapers, books and advertising and developments in photography would remain closely connected, despite the fact that photographs themselves could not be commercially printed alongside text until the last decade of the nineteenth century.

Remarkably, stock blocks continued to be used until the 1970s and beyond, and disappeared only when digital technology finally made letterpress printing itself commercially redundant. The twenty-first century brought with it the digital equivalent of the stock block in the form of clip art.

Fig. 7

Cover of The Illustrated London News, *12 May 1860.*

Fig. 8

A nineteenth-century printer's fist, also known as a mutton fist, digit, manicule, hand director, pointer or pointing hand. The fluid lines suggest that its origin was a pen-and-ink drawing.

517

518

519

520

521

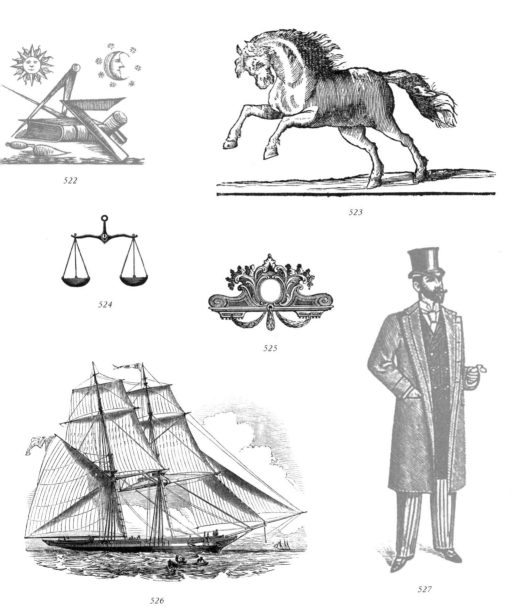

522

523

524

525

526

527

528

529

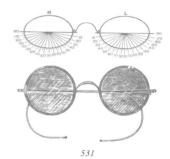

531

530

532

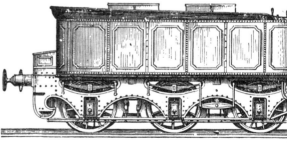

533

534

536

535

537

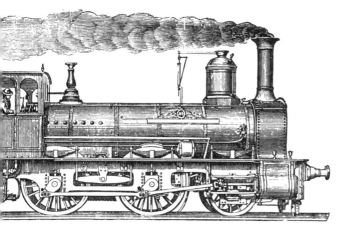

538

539

542

540

541

543

544

545

546

547

548

549

550

551

552

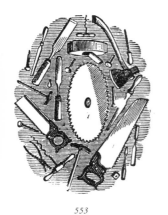

553

554

555

556

557

558

559

560

561

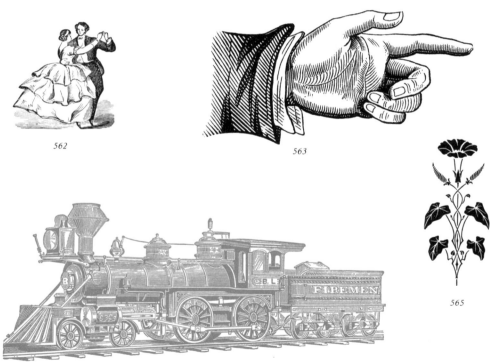

562

563

565

564

566

567

568

569

570

571

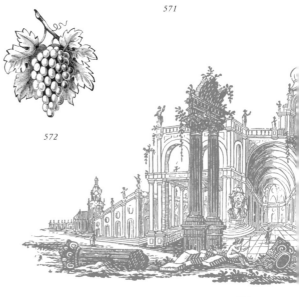

572

573

574

575

576

577

578

579

580

581

584

582

583

585

586

587

588

590

589

591

592

593

594

595

596

597

598

599

600

601

602

603

604

605

606

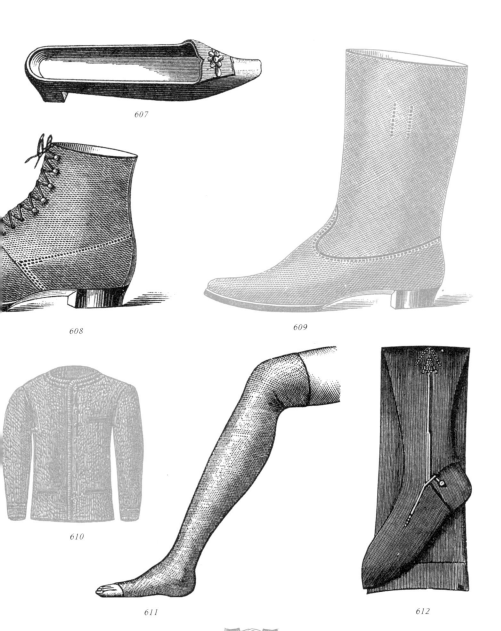

607

608

609

610

611

612

613

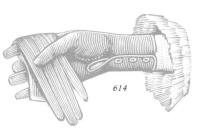

614

615

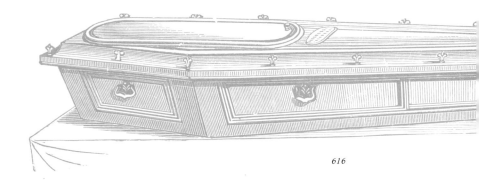

616

617

618

619

620

621

622

623

625

624

626

627

628

630

629

631

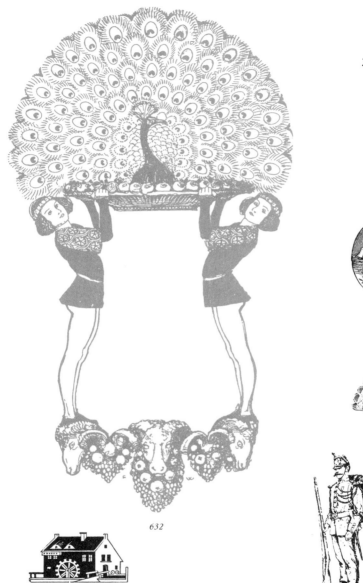

632

634

635

636

637

638

633

639

640

641

642

643

644

645

646

647

648

649

650

651

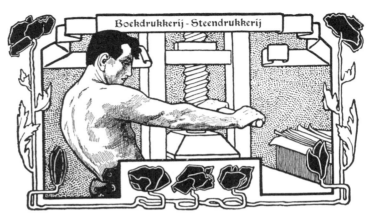

652

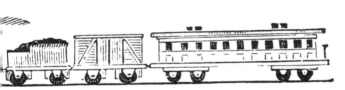

653

654

655

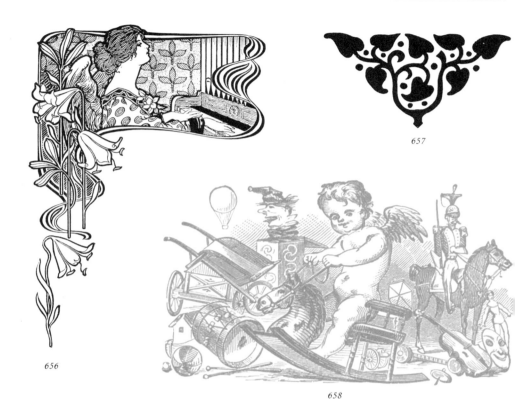

656

657

658

659

660

661

662

664

663

665

666

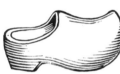

667

668

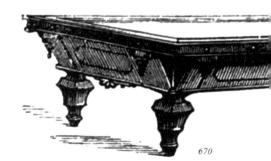

669

670

671

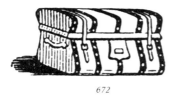

672

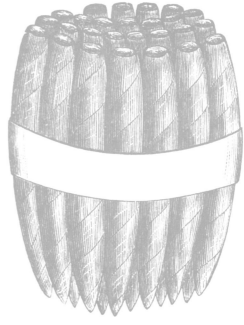

673

674

675

676

677

679

678

680

682

681

683

684

685

686

687

688

689

690

691

692

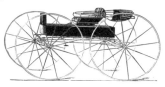

693

694

695

696

697

698

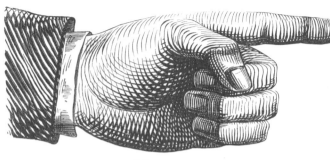

699

700

701

702

703

704

705

706

707

708

709

710

711

712

713

714

715

716

717

718

719

720

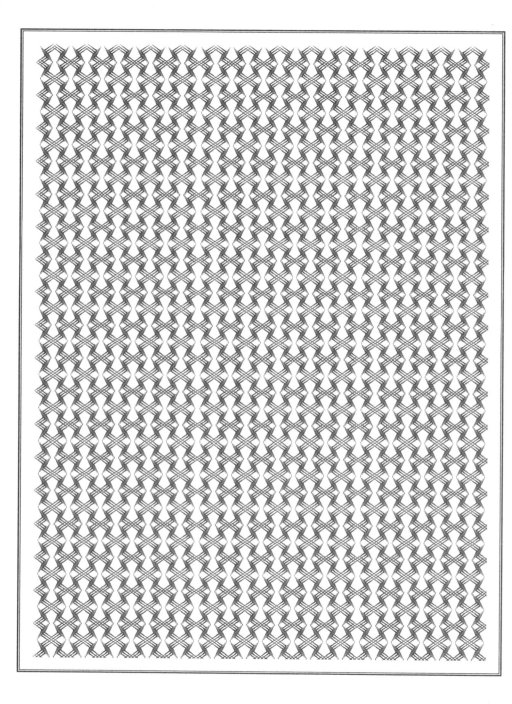

7
Ingenious Art

The twentieth century marked the beginning of the era of the designer. Although the printing industry maintained a 'closed shop' policy (in part as an effort to limit the influence of the designer), it found that its customers were increasingly taking their printing requirements to a designer who then dealt with the printer on their behalf.

During the first two decades of the twentieth century, type foundries continued to sell their fonts and ornaments almost exclusively to the printing industry, but then realized that it was increasingly the designer who was deciding which fonts and ornaments the printer should stock. Some type-foundry directors welcomed this switch of allegiance by the business community from printer to designer.

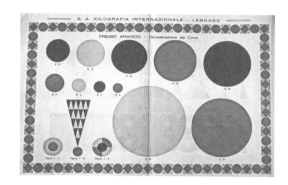

Fig. 1

*A page from a Deberny &
Peignot wood type catalogue,
Paris, c. late 1930s. This edition
published in Italian.
The circles are printed red,
yellow and blue.*

Fig. 2

*Sample setting from the
specimen catalogue of
J.G. Schelter & Giesecke,
Leipzig, 1926. The sans serif
typeface is Koralle.*

Among them was Charles Peignot, co-director of the influential French type foundry Deberny & Peignot, who made public his exasperation at the 'total lack of typographic culture and curiosity in the printing and publishing worlds'.[17] Many leading foundries, Deberny & Peignot included, now adopted the values of the designer and addressed their practical needs through the design and content of their type specimen books (fig. 1).

It was perhaps as part of this re-alignment that type foundries started to commission new fonts from designers of repute working outside the printing and type founding industries, even using the designer's name to help in their promotion. These new fonts aimed to meet the needs of a maturing advertising industry whose designers were, crucially, now being recruited from art colleges and who were hungry for something different with which to work. The simpler forms of the new fonts – often strong, characterful sans serif types – seemed perfect for their needs. Importantly, they were accompanied by ornaments consisting of the most basic of forms: squares, circles and triangles.

These geometric typographic ornaments, the perfect accompaniment to the new sans serif typefaces (fig. 2), really came to the fore when the famous Bauhaus design school in Weimar – and in particular teacher and designer László

Moholy-Nagy – began to incorporate the square, circle and triangle into its printed promotional material (see p. 60, fig. 2). Advocated by acclaimed designers such as Moholy-Nagy, these basic shapes quickly became popular in their own right and, in response, were soon a common sight in German type foundry specimen catalogues (fig. 3). The international trade in foundry type ensured that this promotional material was soon seen in North America, where the style became particularly popular. The combination of simple shapes and primary colours – another Bauhaus-led innovation – transformed advertising and also signalled the beginnings of the independent, professional graphic designer.

The use of these rudimentary shapes as an integral part of the design process was discussed and illustrated in *The American Printer*, December 1927, in an article by Albert Schiller, at that time art director of the Advertising Agencies' Service in New York. He wrote: 'Besides using [typographic ornaments] for illustrations, [German industrialists] have their trademarks designed in this manner, and even students in their trade schools are encouraged to study this ingenious art. For an art it surely is, and needless to say, a direct outgrowth of the German trend toward modernistic expression in design.'

In the same article Schiller emphasizes that it was designers who were choosing to use typographic ornaments to create illustrations, rather than printers: 'I must confess that the majority of printers will miss completely the artistic significance of the result as a "drawing" or design. Their bewilderment will come in when they try to decipher too literally the various elements that make up the whole.' As Schiller intimates, the best examples of typographic pictures are those that do not allude to a direct or realistic representation. Subjects such as buildings might be particularly suitable (and predictable) – given their simple box-like forms (see page 62, fig. 5) – but the most interesting work was that which caused the decorative ornaments

Fig. 3

Cover of the D. Stempel AG specimen catalogue, Frankfurt am Main, 1927.

Fig. 4

Albert Schiller, from his 'Machine-Age Art' exhibition at the New York Public Library, 1952.

themselves to disappear beneath the power of the whole finished image or design.

Only the best of Schiller's work achieves this, although it could be argued that he did more than most to promote the use of typographic ornaments for image making. In 1952 an exhibition of his work called 'Machine-Age Art' was held at the New York Public Library (fig. 4), where, as well as displaying pictures on the walls, he also included large-scale work on the floor, 'formed by placing together mosaic tiles of various size, colour and texture'. The exhibition was followed by a selection of Schiller's work being reproduced in issue no. 36 of *Design and Paper*, the journal of the paper-maker Marquardt & Company Inc., in which Schiller dedicated his work to 'King Bruce of Typelandia', a curious reference to Bruce Rogers.

Other significant designers using typographic ornaments to create images were Georg Goedecker (fig. 5) and Hans Schleger, better known as 'Zero' (fig. 6), who, in the 1930s, produced work commissioned by, among others, London Underground and the General Post Office. For these designers, their work with typographic ornaments has largely been eclipsed by their expansive body of other work. In that sense, they have something in common with the American designer Alvin Lustig, who, more than anyone else, used typographic ornaments to champion Modernist design culture.

From the start, Lustig, like his many predecessors, aimed to set up his own printing and design business from which he could work in his own way and in his own time. With this in mind, in 1933 Lustig attended printing classes run by the fine press printer Richard J. Hoffman, followed by a year at the Art Center School in Los Angeles. After several inauspicious false starts, Lustig was offered a corner in Ward Ritchie's print and publishing company with sufficient space for a desk and his accumulated cases of metal type and ornaments. Lustig called his 'studio' the Media Press. In exchange for the office space and the use of a proofing press,

Lustig designed material for Ritchie as and when required. One of the first things Lustig designed and printed was a specimen sheet to promote his services, and, rather boldly, he explained his approach to design thus, 'From these basic, standard, typographic shapes all the designs shown are constructed, no cuts or drawings being used' (fig. 7).

Lustig transformed typographic ornaments into a highly personal and expressive method of working. He began designing book jackets in the late 1930s, but his best jackets – the 'heroic type pictures' – were designed for Ward Ritchie and James Laughlin's New Directions Books.[18] An abundance of other material, including catalogue and prospectus covers, newsletters, advertising, announcements and greetings cards, as well as becoming the basis of trademarks and logos (such as the masthead of the *Arts and Architecture* magazine, see p. 61, fig. 4), demonstrated Lustig's commitment to typographic ornaments in his formative years (fig. 8).

❧

The Apple Macintosh computer democratized the use of type in the same way that the Kodak Brownie had transformed photography nearly 100 years earlier. For the graphic

Fig. 6

Hans Schleger (adopted the pseudonym 'Zero' in the mid-1920s). Schleger worked in New York and London. Advertisement for Chrysler's Motor Car Co, New York – Berlin, Crawford's Advertising Agency. From 'Gebrauchsgraphic', 1929.

Fig. 7

Alvin Lustig, cover of a self-promotional leaflet displaying his own 'fundamental grammar of visual communication', Los Angeles, 1939.

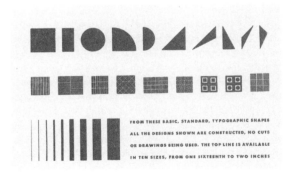

FROM THESE BASIC, STANDARD, TYPOGRAPHIC SHAPES ALL THE DESIGNS SHOWN ARE CONSTRUCTED, NO CUTS OR DRAWINGS BEING USED. THE TOP LINE IS AVAILABLE IN TEN SIZES, FROM ONE SIXTEENTH TO TWO INCHES

Alvin Lustig, Twenty-fifth
Commencement, *for Beverly
Hills High School,
Los Angeles, 1939.*

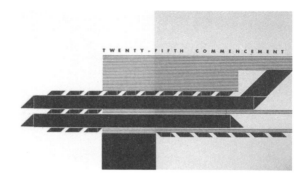

Fig. 9

*Zuzana Licko, sample patterns
constructed from Whirligig,
a 'font' consisting of a series
of decorative units, Berkeley,
California, 1994.*

designer, digital technology offered remarkable flexibility, together with its additional responsibilities, by providing the opportunity to work without recourse to the services of the printer's compositor. The digital innovations of the 1980s also, effectively, marked the end of the type foundry, although a significant few, such as Monotype, managed to make the sizeable leap to digital technology.

Emigre, the journal founded and designed in Berkeley, California, in 1984 by Rudy VanderLans and Zuzana Licko, was one of the earliest, and certainly the most influential, to demonstrate the graphic freedom proffered by digital technology. It was Licko, using FontEditor, who began designing bitmapped fonts, which initially recalled the fascination for geometric forms of the 1920s and Alvin Lustig's experiments in the 1940s. The exposure of Licko's typefaces through the magazine led to the manufacture of Emigre Fonts. It was perhaps inevitable, given *Emigre's* propensity for creative indulgence, that Licko also began to explore the potential of digital typographic ornament. The 61 characters that make up the ornament 'font' Whirligig, utilize the principle of modular construction to create dazzling decorative patterns (fig. 9). Licko's patterns formed by typographic ornaments play a rich and colourful role in the current promotional material of Emigre fonts.

Fig. 10

Restraint, a font designed
by Marian Bantjes in
collaboration with the
typographer Ross Mills,
Vancouver, 2007.

In 2007, the illustrator Marian Bantjes and typographer Ross Mills collaborated on what is, in effect, an ornament font that happens to include letterforms. Restraint (fig. 10) is a typeface built inside out, the letterforms defined by the negative space of the ornament, as if the characters are merely a lucky happenstance. This unconventional font is not for the faint-hearted, but with a little forethought (no more than that required of the letterpress compositor when using printers' flowers) it provides remarkable results, limited only by the 'restraint' shown by the designer.

The typographer Will Hill began work in 2014 on an experimental font called Stochastic (fig. 11), which reflects on the traditions of typographic ornament while using the power and flexibility of digital media. The sharpness and clarity of these designs is reminiscent of early to mid twentieth-century wood-engraved ornaments (see p. 99, fig. 8) and yet they have, in fact, been randomly generated by the application of custom-designed vector brushes to a series of geometric paths.

Fig. 11

Stochastic, an experimental
font by Will Hill, Cambridge,
UK, 2014.

Endnotes

1. This definition of ornament is from James Trilling, *The Language of Ornament*, Thames and Hudson, 2001.

2. Fournier had long planned a four-volume *Manuel Typographique*, but produced only two: *Type, Its Cutting and Founding* in 1764, and *Type Specimens* in 1768. He did not live to complete the other two volumes, one concerned with printing and the other on the lives and work of great typographers.

3. Francis Meynell, a prodigious user and promoter of printers' flowers, and the eminent typographic historian Stanley Morison, described the scarcity of information concerning the origins of printers' flowers as 'unhistorical, indeed almost antihistorical' in their important essay 'Printers' Flowers and Arabesques', *The Fleuron*, no. 1, 1923. This is also included in the *Fleuron Anthology*, edited by Meynell and Herbert Simon, Ernest Benn for the University of Toronto Press, 1973.

4. Bodoni's *Manuale Tipografico* (two volumes), Parma, 1818, published posthumously in a limited edition of 250. Features 142 sets of roman and italic typefaces and a wide selection of borders, ornaments, symbols and flowers, as well as Greek, Hebrew, Russian, Arabic, Phoenician, Armenian, Coptic and Tibetan alphabets.

5. Attempts by the printer to adapt to the commercial opportunities created by the Industrial Revolution is the subject of David Jury, *Graphic Design Before Graphic Designers: The Printer as Designer and Craftsman 1700–1914*, Thames and Hudson, 2012.

6. For a full description of Bruce Rogers' work methods, see Frederic Warde, *Bruce Rogers: Designer of Books*, Harvard University Press, 1925.

7. Francis Meynell and Herbert Simon, introduction to *Fleuron Anthology*, page xi, Ernest Benn for the University of Toronto Press, 1973.

8. William A. Dwiggins, 'New Kinds of Printing Calls for New Design', *Boston Evening Transcript*, Graphic Arts Section, 29 August 1922.

9. Philip B. Meggs and Alston W. Purvis, *Meggs' History of Graphic Design*, Chapter 8, John Wiley & Sons, 2013.

10. Monotype made two different versions of Fournier. Fournier series 185, a lighter, slightly condensed typeface, is the version that came to be referred to by the print trade as Fournier. The second, slightly bolder, more robust version was given the name Barbou. See Allen Hutt, *Fournier: The Compleat Typographer*, pp. 75–6, Rowman and Littlefield, 1972.

11. Multiple rules were two or more lines of the same or differing widths of printing surface on the same body. The body of a rule was normally not less than 1.5 points wide, so that rules of less than this width, when set side by side, had some space between them.

12. See Crispin Elsted and David Jury, *Bordering on the Sublime: Ornamental Typography at the Curwen Press*, Barbarian Press, 2015 (estimated publication date).

13. For a more detailed explanation of the technical processes involved, see Anthony Dyson, *Pictures to Print: The Nineteenth-century Engraving Trade*, Farrand Press, London, 1984.

14. Doug Clouse, *MacKellar, Smiths & Jordan: Typographic Tastemakers of the Late Nineteenth Century*, Oak Knoll Press, 2008.

15. Michael Twyman, *Printing 1770–1970*, p. 95, British Library, 1998.

16. Jury, *Graphic Design before Graphic Designers*, pp. 118–19.

17. Charles Peignot, *Divertissements Typographiques*, no. 1, Deberny & Peignot type foundry, Paris, 1928.

18. Ward Ritchie in conversation with Elaine Lustig Cohen in 1982. Quoted in Steven Heller and Elaine Lustig Cohen, *Born Modern: The Life and Design of Alvin Lustig*, p. 43, Chronicle Books, 2010.

Acknowledgements

With thanks to the following for making material from their personal collections available: John Ellis, Justin Knopp, Richard Sheaff, Sullivan Bindery, Michael Taylor, Brian Webb and David Wakefield.

Picture Credits

David Jury is the author of a number of books including *New Typographic Design* (Laurence King), *Graphic Design Before Graphic Designers* (Thames and Hudson), *Letterpress: The Allure of the Handmade* (RotoVision) and numerous articles on typography, printing and graphic design. From 1996 to 2006 he was the editor of *TypoGraphic* (the journal of the International Society of Typographic Designers). Jury also designs, prints and publishes limited edition letterpress books for his own Fox Ash Studio Press, many of which are in public collections including the Yale Centre for British Art, USA, and the Museum Van Het Boek, Holland. He was course leader of MA studies in 'Art, Design, and the Book' at Colchester School of Art from 2007 to 2012, and currently teaches 'Typographic Enquiry' on the MA Typography course at Anglia Ruskin University, Cambridge.

www.davidjury.com